Fair Pl

Ella Roa

methuen | drama

LONDON • NEW YORK • OXFORD • NEW DELHI • SYDNEY

METHUEN DRAMA
Bloomsbury Publishing Plc
50 Bedford Square, London, WC1B 3DP, UK
1385 Broadway, New York, NY 10018, USA
29 Earlsfort Terrace, Dublin 2, Ireland

BLOOMSBURY, METHUEN DRAMA and the Methuen
Drama logo are trademarks of Bloomsbury Publishing Plc

First published in Great Britain 2021

A catalogue record for this book is available from the British Library.

A catalog record for this book is available from the Library of Congress.

ISBN: PB: 978-1-3502-9162-1
ePDF: 978-1-3502-9163-8
eBook: 978-1-3502-9164-5

Series: Modern Plays

Typeset by Mark Heslington Ltd, Scarborough, North Yorkshire
Printed and bound in Great Britain

To find out more about our authors and books visit
www.bloomsbury.com and sign up for our newsletters.

Fair Play

by Ella Road

Credits

Ann | NicK King

Sophie | Charlotte Beaumont

Playwright | Ella Road

Director | Monique Touko

Set and Costume Designer | Naomi Dawson

Lighting Designer | Matt Haskins

Sound Designer and Composer | Giles Thomas

Movement Director | Joseph Toonga

Assistant Movement Director | Orin 'oriyo' Norbert

Costume Supervisor | Megan Rarity

Casting Director | Heather Basten CDG

Casting Assistant | Fran Cattaneo

Production Manager | Jerome Reid

CSM | Kala Simpson

ASM | Emily Mei-Ling Pearce

Stage Management Placement | Sam Marshall

Associate Producer | Sonia Friedman Productions

Cast

Sophie | Charlotte Beaumont

Charlotte Beaumont's theatre credits include: *The Lovely Bones* (Birmingham Repertory Theatre and UK tour); *The Importance of Being Earnest* (The Watermill); *Romeo and Juliet* (The Globe); *No One Will Tell Me How to Start A Revolution* (Hampstead Theatre); *Jumpy* (Theatre Clwyd); *Three Winters* (National Theatre, Lyttleton); *Playhouse Creatures* (Chichester Festival Theatre); *The Flooded Grave* and *2,000 Feet Away* (The Bush Theatre). On television she has appeared in *Broadchurch* (ITV); *Waterloo Road* (BBC); *Death in Paradise* (BBC); *Coming Up: Sink or Swim* (Channel 4); *Zapped* (Baby Cow); and *Skins* (E4). Charlotte's film appearances include: *The Windmill Massacre* (Pellicola); *Butterfly Kisses* (Blue Shadow Films); *Balcony* (Clipside Films); *Skip Girl* (Mara Adina); *Jupiter Ascending* (Warner Bros); *Tommy* (Left Bank Pictures); and *Sex & Drugs & Rock & Roll* (Aegis Film Fund).

Ann | NicK King

With roots in Broadway, network television and both voice and commercial acting, NicK King's previous stage credits include the thirtieth anniversary USA tour of *Annie*, *The Lion King* (Broadway) and *The Nutcracker* (The Washington Ballet). NicK has appeared on television in *Law & Order* and *Village People* and in the short films *Dead Air* and *FINE* as well as regional and national US commercials.

NicK is no newcomer to storytelling from the heart, having written their own stories in the forms of a published book of poetry and prose, songs, series, and stage plays.

With new opportunities emerging for intersex, trans/nonbinary and queer actors every day, NicK is eager to contribute to creating and telling stories that explore all sides of them and their surrounding communities.

Playwright | Ella Road

Ella Road's debut play *The Phlebotomist* was produced at
Hampstead Theatre, directed by Sam Yates. It was nominated
for an Olivier Award and was a finalist for the Susan Smith
Blackburn Prize. It was translated into a radio drama for BBC
Radio 3 and is now being adapted for screen. Ella is currently
writing new plays for the Almeida Theatre and Hampstead
Theatre. Her play *How to Eat an Elephant* was due to premiere
at Theatre Royal Plymouth last year and has been postponed
due to the pandemic. Ella recently finished writing on the
British series of *Call My Agent* for Bron/Headline, for which she
wrote two episodes. She is currently writing projects for the
BBC and Film4, and developing original series with Drama
Republic, Potboiler and Element Pictures. Ella was lucky
enough to be a Soho Theatre Young Writer 2017/18, one of the
Bush Theatre's Emerging Writers 2018/19, and on the BBC
Drama Writersroom 2019/20. Ella is part of the London
Theatre Consortium's Climate Lab, looking at how we can
move to more sustainable working practices in the industry.
She also facilitates theatre workshops in prisons with Synergy
Theatre.

Director | Monique Touko

Director Monique Touko made her professional debut with
Malindadzimu by Mufuro Makubika at Hampstead Theatre
Downstairs. Her directing training included the Regional
Theatre Young Directors Scheme at Royal Exchange
Manchester and at the Young Vic, her training involved the
Intro to Directing course led by Sasha Wares, Boris Karloff
Trainee Assistant Directors Programme and the Jerwood
Assistant Director Scheme.

Her assisting credits include: *Wishlist* by Katherine Soper,
directed by Matthew Xia at Royal Exchange Manchester and
Royal Court, HighTides' touring production of *Kanye the First*
by Sam Steiner directed by Andrew Twyman, *Yellowman* by Dael
Orlandersmith directed by Nancy Medina at Young Vic, *China*

Plate's on the Exhale by Martin Zimmerman directed by Christopher Haydon at Traverse Theatre, *Cock* by Mike Bartlett directed by Kate Hewitt at Chichester Festival Theatre, Shakespeare's *Richard II* directed Lynette Linton and Adjoa Andoh at Shakespeare's Globe Theatre, Ibsen's *Rosmersholm* adapted by Duncan Macmillan, directed by Ian Rickson at Duke of York Theatre and Lorca's *Blood Wedding* adapted by Marina Carr directed by Yael Farber at Young Vic.

She is also part of The Ubunifu Space which is an online platform that builds and raises the profiles of creative artists within Africa. Monique is Partnership Manager and Assistant Producer for Ubunifu Radio as well as a regular member of the UK reaction team on the YouTube channel which has a global following of 300K+ subscribers.

Set and Costume Designer | Naomi Dawson

Training: Wimbledon School of Art and Kunstacademie, Maastricht.

Recent theatre design credits include: *Romeo and Juliet*, *As You Like It* (Regent's Park); *Whole* (Arcola and national tour); *Twelfth Night* (Guthrie Theater, US); *Scenes with Girls*, *The Woods* (Royal Court); *Light Falls*, *Happy Days* (Royal Exchange, Manchester); *The Convert*, *The Container* (Young Vic); *The Duchess of Malfi*, *Doctor Faustus*, *The White Devil*, *The Roaring Girl* (RSC); *The Tin Drum* (Kneehigh/Liverpool Everyman); *Gaslight*, *Care* (Watford Palace); *The Winter's Tale* (Romateatern, Sweden); *Beryl* (West Yorkshire Playhouse/UK tour); *Kasimir and Karoline*, *Fanny and Alexander* (Malmo Stadsteater, Sweden); *Every One* (Battersea Arts Centre); *Weaklings* (Warwick Arts/UK tour); *Brave New World* (Royal & Derngate, Northampton/UK tour); *Men in the Cities* (Royal Court/Traverse Theatre/UK tour); *Hotel*, *Three More Sleepless Nights* (National Theatre); *Wildefire* (Hampstead).

Opera include: *Die Frau Ohne Schatten* (covid postponed; Dutch National Opera); *Madama Butterfly* (Grimeborn, Arcola); *The Lottery*, *The Fairy Queen* (Bury Court Opera).

Lighting Designer | Matt Haskins

Matt's work ranges from lighting the icon Grace Jones in Concert (Royal Albert Hall); working as Associate Lighting Designer for *The Master and Margarita* (Complicité – world tour); the Royal Opera House world premiere of Neil Gaiman's *Coraline*; and the award-winning West End production of *Peter Pan Goes Wrong* (Australia, Italy, Mexico, NZ and UK tours).

Theatre: *The Witchfinder's Sister* (Queen's Theatre Hornchurch); *The System* (Original Theatre Company); *Folk, Malindadzimu, Raya* (Hampstead Downstairs); *Zorro* (Hope Mill Theatre); *The Lovely Bones* (Birmingham Rep, UK tour); *Hobson's Choice* (Royal Exchange); *Cost of Living, I and You* (Hampstead Theatre); *Nina – A Story About Me and Nina Simone* (Young Vic).

Opera: Ravi Shankar's *Sukanya* (ROH/Royal Festival Hall); *Turn of the Screw, The Snowmaiden, Hansel and Gretel, La Traviata, Don Giovanni* (Opera North); *Roméo et Juliette* (Estonian National Opera); *Albert Herring* (Maggio Musicale Fiorentino).

Sound Designer and Composer | Giles Thomas

Giles received a BA (Hons) in Sound Technology from the Liverpool Academy for Performing Arts.

He has worked as a composer and sound designer for theatre for over a decade as well as time spent as a music producer and mix engineer.

Movement Director | Joseph Toonga

Joseph Toonga originates from Cameroon and is Artistic Director of Just Us Dance Theatre and Artists 4 Artists.

He makes dance productions relevant to the here and now and his craftsmanship and signature choreographic style challenges conventions commonly used in Hip Hop dance and shifts audience perceptions by addressing racial stigmas and societal stereotypes.

Joseph has recently been appointed Emerging Choreographer with the Royal Ballet, his commissions and achievements to date include: Secret Cinema collaboration for premier of French film *Les Misérables*, DanceEast Associate Artist, Boston Conservatoire of Dance, National Youth Ballet/ Bundesjugendballett, Richard Alston Dance Company, Elephant in the Black Box, Junior Ballet Madrid, East Wall with Hofesh ShechterBest Choreography Award Reverb Dance Festival (New York).

Assistant Movement Director | Orin 'oriyo' Norbert

Orin 'oriyo' Norbert is a creative artist, composer and DJ. Starting out in 2001 as a dancer, choreographer and director, Orin has worked and performed across the UK and Europe on multimedia projects in dance, art and film. As a producer and performer his credits include: BBC Blast Dance National Finalist (2006). Lead actor: 'Juice' in the Royal Opera House's production *Demon Juice* (2007). Co-choreographer and Musical Director: 'I AM' by PRYOR (Breakin' Convention – 2008). Singer: Boney M (tribute tour – Prague 2009).

Founder: OMG Collective (2013); Alternative R&B outfit featured on BBC, Kiss FM Australia and Jazz FM. Performer: *Obibini* by Kwame Asafo-Adjei (Sadlers Wells, 2018).

As a composer and creative support, Orin has been involved with various theatre and hip-hop theatre projects such as 'Daughter, Daughter' (Just Us Dance Theatre, 2017–18); 'SEAN' (Chris Reyes, 2019); 'N9NE' (Ashley J Francis, 2021) and CARAVAN Social Night; where he currently serves as a Musical Director and Resident Artist.

Casting Director | Heather Basten CDG

Heather Basten is an English casting director based in London, and a member of the Casting Directors Guild (UK), and the Casting Society of America (USA). In 2021 she was recognised as a Screen International 'Star of Tomorrow'.

As well as casting *Fair Play* for The Bush Theatre, Heather has also cast the upcoming 6-episode musical TV series *Jungle* for

Amazon Studios and *Dreaming Whilst Black* for the BBC. She has most recently cast the Stone Age-set film *The Origin*, which is the newest sophomore feature from UK producer Oliver Kassman (*Saint Maud*).

Heather is currently casting a new exciting slate of green-lit films across the BFI, Blumhouse, Film 4 and the BBC, and casting more theatre for The Bush. Heather is assisted by Fran Cattaneo.

Sonia Friedman Productions

SONIA FRIEDMAN PRODUCTIONS (SFP), has developed, initiated and produced over 170 productions and the company has won a staggering 58 Olivier Awards, 34 Tonys and 2 BAFTAs.

In 2019, Sonia Friedman OBE was awarded 'Producer of the Year' at the Stage Awards for a record breaking fourth time. In 2018, Friedman was also featured in TIME 100 and in 2017 she took the number one spot in 'The Stage 100', becoming the first number one in the history of the compilation not to own or operate West End theatres and the first solo woman for almost 20 years.

Current productions include: the UK premiere of *The Book of Mormon*, West End, UK and European Tour, *Harry Potter and the Cursed Child* in London, New York, Melbourne, San Francisco and Hamburg, *Mean Girls* US Tour, *The Shark is Broken*, West End and the world premiere of Tom Stoppard's *Leopoldstadt* (Wyndham's Theatre, London).

TV productions include BBC's *Wolf Hall*, *The Dresser* and *King Lear* with Anthony Hopkins, *Uncle Vanya*, *J'Ouvert* and Dennis Kelly's *Together*, with James McAvoy and Sharon Horgan.

Bush Theatre

We make theatre for London. Now.

The Bush is a world-famous home for new plays and an internationally renowned champion of playwrights. We discover, nurture and produce the best new writers from the widest range of backgrounds from our home in a distinctive corner of West London.

Bush Theatre, 7 Uxbridge Road, London W12 8LJ
Box Office: 020 8743 5050 | Administration: 020 8743 3584
Email: info@bushtheatre.co.uk
bushtheatre.co.uk

Alternative Theatre Company Ltd
The Bush Theatre is a Registered Charity and a company limited by guarantee.
Registered in England no. 1221968 Charity no. 270080

THANK YOU

The Bush Theatre would like to thank all its supporters whose valuable contributions have helped us to create a platform for our future and to promote the highest quality new writing, develop the next generation creative talent, lead innovative community engagement work and champion diversity.

MAJOR DONORS
Gianni & Michael Alen-Buckley
Charles Holloway
Georgia Oetker
Tim & Cathy Score
Susie Simkins

LONE STARS
Gianni Alen-Buckley
Michael Alen-Buckley
Jacqui Bull
Rafael & Anne-Helene Biosse Duplan
Charles Holloway
Priscilla John
Rosemary Morgan
Georgia Oetker
Jack Thorne

HANDFUL OF STARS
Charlie Bigham
Judy Bollinger
Clyde Cooper
Sue Fletcher
Joanna Kennedy
Simon & Katherine Johnson
Garry Lawrence
V&F Lukey
Anthony Marraccino
Aditya Mittal
Robert Ledger & Sally Moulsdale
Clare Rich
Dame Emma Thompson
Kit and Anthony Van Tulleken

RISING STARS
David Brooks
Catharine Browne
Matthew Byam Shaw
Philip Cameron & Richard Smith
Esperanza Cerdan
Grace Chan
Lauren Clancy
Tim & Andrea Clark
Richard & Sarah Clarke
Susie Cuff
Matthew Cushen
Philippa Dolphin
Jack Gordon & Kate Lacy
Hugh & Sarah Grootenhuis
Thea Guest
Lesley Hill & Russ Shaw
Fiona I'Anson
Melanie Johnson
Davina & Malcolm Judelson
Lynette Linton
Miggy Littlejohns
Michael McCoy
Judith Mellor
Caro Millington
Danny Morrison
Dan & Laurie Mucha
Raj & Kim Parkash
Mark & Anne Paterson
Joe Tinston & Amelia Knott
Peter Tausig
Jan Topham
Guy Vincent & Sarah Mitchell

CORPORATE SPONSORS
Biznography
Jamie Lloyd Company
U+I
White Light
Wychwood Media

TRUSTS AND FOUNDATIONS
29th May 1961 Charitable Trust
Boris Karloff Foundation
Christina Smith Foundation
Cockayne Foundation Grants for the Arts
The Daisy Trust
Esmee Fairbairn
Hammersmith United Charities
The Harold Hyam Wingate Foundation
John Lyon's Charity
Leche Trust
Orange Tree Trust
Royal Victoria Hall Foundation
The Teale Charitable Trust
Tesco Bags of Help
Tudor Trust
Victoria Wood Foundation
Weinstock Fund

And all the donors who wish to remain anonymous.

bushtheatre.co.uk

Supported by
ARTS COUNCIL ENGLAND

If you are interested in finding out how to be involved, please visit **bushtheatre.co.uk/support-us** or email **eleanortindall@bushtheatre.co.uk** or call **020 8743 3584**.

Fair Play

Cast

Ann, *Nigerian-British. 17 up to 19ish. Athletic.*
Sophie, *White-British. 18 up to 20ish. Athletic.*

A Note on the Play

The story carries us swiftly through time and space. It is inherently physical and playful. Set should be simple. Props minimal or non-existent. This is a play about bodies: their capabilities, limits, and idiosyncrasies; the boundaries we impose on them, and their tendency to misbehave.

A Note on Form

Each scene is like a 'rep' in a training session.

Sophie and Ann each have a stop-clock, which corresponds to them. At the beginning of each scene their clocks begin; when they end the scene their clocks stop.

This might not happen at the same time for each of them, depending on who has 'won' the rep.

Sometimes it might not happen at all.

A Note on the Text

/ indicates an interruption.

. . . indicates a broken or unfinished thought.

NB: *some edits were made to the performance text in response to casting to accommodate accent, dialect and some other details. After all, theatre is and should be a responsive process. A copy of the text as performed is available via agent upon request.*

In Solidarity

With Annet, Dutee, Caster, Francine, Margaret, Pinki, Christine, Beatrice, and the many more whose names I do not know.

With Thanks

To Payoshni Mitra and Holly Greenberry for their invaluable insight and expertise.

To the entire Bush team who supported this play into being with such love and patience, in particular to Dee, Ifrah and Jess, who were there from the start.

To every single wonderful creative who has given their time, energy and skill to the process over development and production in particular to Charley, NicK, Adeyinka and – of course – Monique.

To my old running coaches Nina, Geoff, Jerry and Kabir for their care and inspiration; and to Pete Scott, who loves athletics more than anyone I know.

And, of course, to my amazing family and friends . . . for keeping me bouncing.

Never slow down for the world. One day it will catch up with you.

– Caster Semenya

Prologue

Ann *and* Sophie *enter, ready to run.*

Ann *is nervous.* Sophie *is not. But both exude the powerful vulnerability of athletes in their prime, balancing on a knife edge between success and failure.*

The girls move towards their starting positions, limbering up, stretching and checking shoe-laces. They jump up and down – pumping themselves up.

Their clocks both re-set to '00.00'.

The girls take their marks: pure focus. A starting gun: BANG! And /

1

Athletics track. Post-collision. Out of breath.

Sophie Stay in your / lane!

Ann I'm so, / so

Sophie / Jesus

Ann Sorry /, I'm

Sophie Christ /

Ann Sorry, I didn't / see you

Sophie You ran *right* into me, you / literally

Ann Yeah, no, sorry I was / just

Sophie You have to *look* before crossing the / inside lane

Ann I know. / Sorry.

Sophie You've just fucked up my rep. Fucked it.

Sophie *bends to catch her breath.*

Ann Sorry, I was just, I wasn't looking where I was / going

Sophie   You're lucky I didn't run straight into you.

Beat.

Ann   You were going proper fast on that one. Looking proper strong.

Pause. Sophie's breath slows.

Sophie   I've never seen you before.

Ann   No, I. First session, my first time down here, / so

Sophie *checks the time.*

Sophie   I've got one more rep. Keep out of the inside lane.

Ann   Well I got another set, three hundreds, we're using lane one as well, / so

Sophie   I mean when you're not running. Obviously.

Ann   Oh. Right. Sure. Sorry . . . Again.

Beat.

You're Sophie King, right?

Sophie   Yeah.

Ann   I'm . . .

But /

2

Track outbuildings. Post-session. Cold.

Ann   Um. Sorry. D'you know where I can get some / water?

Sophie   Good session.

Ann   Oh. Oh, cheers.

Sophie   You were right up in the mix.

Ann   Only on the last one. And it's just C-group, innit.

Sophie Better than D-group.

Ann *Is* there a D-group?

Sophie No. But you're here aren't you?

Ann Ha. Yeah. No yeah, I mean . . . *yeah*. / Ha.

Sophie 800 metres?

Ann *nods.*

Sophie Me too.

Ann Yeah, I know. I mean obviously, I mean I saw you race up in Glasgow? You slayed it! You were / amazing

Sophie Oh / thanks

Ann I mean I didn't actually *see* you see you, I mean like I watched online. Such an incredible race, man, the way you just *kicked*! So tactical, like so / impressive

Sophie Where did Paul poach you from?

Ann Well, he didn't exactly poach / me

Sophie Like 'scout' then, whatever.

Ann English Schools? But Mum wouldn't let me join, like she wanted me to do first term of A-levels first, / so

Sophie I meant like . . . where did you transfer from?

Ann Oh! Richmond AC?

Sophie You from there then? Richmond?

Ann No, well I'm . . . I'm from . . . Well, Nigerian actually, like I was born in Nigeria, / then

Sophie Oh, no, sorry I meant, I literally, sorry, I just meant like where do you . . . live?

Ann Oh! Ha. We're in like . . . Hounslow?

Sophie Hounslow? That's, where is that? That's . . .

Ann   West London? / It's

Sophie   That's *far*.

Ann   Yeah.

Sophie   You travel down here *every* session?!

Ann   Well, gonna see how it goes.

Sophie   Nigeria. That's cool. When did you move here?

Ann   Oh, when I was tiny. Mum's got a bunch of family here, so.

Beat.

Sophie   Ann, right? Ann Ayaba?

Ann   'Ayaba'

Sophie   'Ann Ayaba'.

Beat.

If you go in there there's a fountain on the left.

Ann   Oh! Right. Cool, thanks.

Sophie   Water tastes like shit though. There's a vending machine, but don't buy the blue gatorade.

Ann   Yeah ha no that stuff's *nasty*.

Sophie   No, it's just there's only one left and I want it.

Ann   Oh. Sorry.

Then /

3

Track. Mid-session. Bent, out of breath.

Ann   How many are we doing?

Sophie   He said, 8 / to 12

Ann But / like

Sophie As many as you can.

Sophie *stands to go again.* Ann *tries to, but /*

Ann Think I'm gonna be /

And /

4

Post-session.

Sophie You should warm down the other way, even up your legs.

Ann I'm gonna do a couple more laps if / you wanna

Sophie I said I'd wait for Dan.

Ann Dan?

Sophie Steeple-chaser Dan. Like / tall, skinny

Ann Oh, your boyfriend.

Sophie *No.* Eugh why does *everyone* think we're a thing? He's not my boyfriend, he's my *training buddy*.

Squinting across the track.

Paul's eyeballing us.

Ann *looks over. Straightens.* Sophie *stands, and shouts across.*

Sophie I'm gonna warm down in a sec! I'm just waiting for Dan!

Sophie *shivers. Turns back.*

Eugh where *is he*? I bet he's having a shit, I told him that Swedish recovery drink was a laxative.

Ann *laughs. Looks across the track. Shivers too.*

Ann I gotta catch the bus, so.

Sophie   Well OK, bye then.

And /

5

Trackside. Post-session. Stretching.

Sophie   Then you probably weren't running fast enough.

Ann   I meant, I just *meant* it was a short / session

Sophie   Lactic threshold work is all about precision. It's quality not quantity.

Ann   Ha, you sound like coach.

Sophie   No I don't. Anyway, Paul knows what he's doing.

Ann smiles.

Sophie   What?

Ann   Why d'you call him Paul?

Sophie   Coz that's his name.

Ann   Everyone else calls him 'coach'.

Sophie   Well I call him Paul. Anyway, even if you can't feel it, you'll be lactic. You were up there with Jackie, you were going fast.

Ann   Thought you said I wasn't going fast enough.

Sophie   No, I . . . you said that, I said . . . Look I don't know how fast you were going, do I? I mean, what were you repping?

Ann   Um 25s at the start, last set 24s?

Sophie   You were repping sub 25s?

Ann   Only on the last four.

Beat. Sophie *tries not to look impressed. Then /*

MOVEMENT

Training. And /

Scene Six

Mid-session. Hot.

Sophie   S'not a 'go', it's called a 'rep'?

Ann   A rep, / yeah

Sophie   Yeah.

Ann   Yeah, I know that, I'm not dumb / you know

Sophie   No, it's just you kept calling it / a

Ann   Yeah, does it matter?

Sophie   Sorry.

And /

7

Hallway. Ann *leaning, upset.*

Ann   Like I *care*, obviously I wanna get fast, but I can't think about it every second, can I? I got college and stuff. He doesn't get it. He keeps being like 'Focus . . . Focus, Ann. It's up to you, Ann'. I am focused. Anyways like if it's up to me, then why's he shouting?

Sophie   He wasn't shouting. Trust / me

Ann   All I said was, I just told him I'll miss hills on Saturday coz my Dad's in town, right, and he's / all

Sophie   Well, why can't you just see him after training?

Ann   No, we, argh! *No!* We're doing a big lunch thing, family thing, I gotta help Mum cook. And he's all like 'Well it's up to you, Ann'. He's so weird, how he talks, like a robot, all dead-pan. And his breath always smells like old / milk

Sophie   Don't be rude.

Ann   It does. All nasty, sour kinda / milky

Sophie   He spends ages drawing up our programmes. A lot of thought goes into it. So if you don't follow it properly, he gets upset. If he's pushing, it's coz he cares. Coz he sees potential. Otherwise he wouldn't bother. Anyway he's not your teacher. You don't have to be here.

Ann *nearly retorts, but* Sophie *moves off, and /*

MOVEMENT

They train. Sophie *focussed.* Ann *straining. And /*

8

Car park. Cold.

Sophie   But it's *freezing*. We can go past the station.

Ann   Gotta finish my homework on the bus. Got like a whole comprehension for tomorrow / so

Sophie   What on?

Ann   *Jane Eyre?*

Sophie   Ewh. I did that. It's sooo long. Well, it's not 'long', but it's like, *long*, you know. You coming to camp? Pre-season training camp? At Easter?

Ann   Er /

Sophie   Paul might ask you. Reckon he will. You're pretty good.

Ann   Cheers.

Sophie   If he asks you should come. It's great / training

Ann   Yeah, no he did already ask.

Sophie   Oh. Well come then! It's in Lanzarote. I did it last year, it's super fun. And they've like, got bursaries if / you

Ann   Yeah, I know.

Sophie   Well / then

Ann *shivers, gesturing to the car.*

Ann   Isn't your mum waiting / for

Sophie   She doesn't mind.

Ann   Look I'm gonna miss the . . .

Ann *backs away.* Sophie *opens her mouth, and /*

9

Lanzarote. Ann *squints in the hot sun.*

Ann   So what do we do now? Coach said training at 5, yeah?

Sophie   I dunno. Unpack. Sunbathe. Watch telly. I'm going swimming.

Ann *looks around. A beat, then /*

10

Track. Lanzarote. Mid-session. Breathless.

Sophie   Well then take your top off! Look, Sara's got hers off. And Lyds.

Ann   I just . . .

Sophie   You've got great abs, don't fish.

Ann   Huh?

Sophie   I'm not gonna say it again.

Ann   No, it's not that, / I . . .

Sophie   It's no different to wearing a bikini.

Ann *shrugs*.

Sophie   Well then don't moan about being hot.

Ann   I wasn't *moaning*, I was . . .

Sophie *lifts up* Ann's *top and whacks her belly*.

Ann   Hey. Hey! No. Stop it!

Sophie   See?! Abs. For. Days.

Ann *yanks her top back down, annoyed, then /*

11

Trackside. Lanzarote.

Ann   I'm *fine*.

Sophie   Why did you huff off then?

Ann   You know why! Lydia elbowed me didn't she?

Sophie *makes a face*.

Ann   *She did!* On the last rep, here, it's gonna leave / a

Sophie   Well, I'm sure she didn't do it on purpose.

Ann   *She did*.

Sophie   But why would / she

Ann   Maybe coz she doesn't like me over-taking her? She's been throwing me shade all week.

Beat.

Sophie   Paul gave her a right bollocking. She's crying. Look.

She looks across the track. Ann *glances over*.

Sophie   You didn't have to snitch.

Ann   I just asked her why she did it! It proper hurt. She's got real boney arms. Spiky.

Sophie   That's not funny.

Ann   What?

Sophie   She's bulimic.

Ann   Oh.

Sophie   Look, it's always messy on the line, you just have to watch out. Know your spot. Stay in lane. Keep your elbows / in

Ann   She's gotta keep *her* elbows in.

Sophie   Do you want sympathy or not?

Ann   You're not giving me any sympathy!

Sophie   I came to see if you were OK.

Ann   No you didn't.

Beat.

Sophie   Anyway we got circuits in ten.

Ann   What? Now?!

Ann *flops, rubs her legs.*

What time's lunch?

Sophie   1.15.

Ann   Eugh, I'm *starving*. It's like being in prison.

Beat.

If I have to eat another bowl of spaghetti Bolognese . . .

Sophie   It's chilli con carne today.

Ann   Same thing.

Beat.

Sophie   Look. We've got two weeks here right. If you want people to like you just . . . don't be a snitch.

Ann   Yeah, and if you want me to like you, don't be a bitch.

Sophie *opens her mouth but* Ann *walks away . . . then /*

MOVEMENT

Training. Sophie *poised;* Ann *exhausted, until /*

12

Hotel grounds. Sophie *laughing.* Ann *not.*

Sophie   Sorry! Sorry we, um, sorry I was just, haaa basically we all snuck into Dan's room, and we've been . . . basically We saw you from the balcony and Suz dared me to sneak up / on

Ann   Oh.

Sophie   Sorry I scared you.

Ann   Nah, I saw your shadow. Heard everyone laughing.

Ann *glances up at the balcony.* Sophie *does too.*

Sophie   It's just silly. Like truth or dare. Like apart from Mo having to kiss Sean it's actually just been kind of silly, like nothing gross. Wanna come and play?

Beat.

Why you out here in the dark?

Ann   I'm trying to call my mum. Can't do it in my room can I. Sara's in there.

Sophie   Oh *course*, you're sharing with *Sara*. I shared with her last year. *Never stops talking.*

Ann   Yeah, like I don't wanna be rude, but is it a condition?

Sophie   Haahaa, she's just anxious, I dunno. Does she still listen to story-tapes?! I swear I had Stephen Fry going round my head literally the whole camp. Like running around, like, on your marks, set: 'Harry, Ron and Hermione . . .'

Ann *chuckles. Beat.*

Sophie   You nervous about tomorrow?

Ann *shrugs. Nods.*

Sophie   Me too. Everyone is. Trust me. But it doesn't mean anything. It's just to see how we're doing. Just a time trial. It's not a big deal. Seriously it's not.

Ann   It kind of is.

Sophie   It's not.

Ann   It is if I wanna keep my bursary.

Beat. Then . . .

MOVEMENT

Pre-race routine: Ann *touches her cross;* Sophie *arches her back. Then BANG! And /*

13

Changing rooms.

Sophie   Look, it doesn't count.

Ann   So your PB doesn't count then?

Sophie   No, I mean pressure's off, it's just practice / for

Ann   Exactly, and if I can't even do *this* then . . .

Sophie   You were only like *half a second* off your / PB!

Ann   Yeah, but I *know* I can go faster, *I know I can*. I'm not even tired, my legs are fine, I could literally go out there and run it again! It's the start, I messed up the / start!

Sophie   You did / fine

Ann   Stop being nice to me!

Sophie *looks at her for a beat, turns to go.*

Ann   Sorry. Sorry, sorry I'm sorry, I'm just . . . I get shook. My brain, aaah, on the line it's like something kicks in, a voice here like 'why do you even think you can do this?'.

Sophie   Well if it's just some voice then tell it to shut the fuck up and stop being so negative.

Ann   But / I

Sophie   Just tell it to shut up. Like this. 'Shut the fuck up.'

Ann   But /

Sophie   'Shut the fuck up.' You did fine. It's a pre-season trial. You'll do better next time. I'm gonna go warm down.

Sophie *moves off and /*

14

Gym. Strength and conditioning.

Sophie   You smell nice.

Ann   Huh?

Sophie   *You smell nice.*

Ann   No I / don't

Sophie   You do. All sweet. You always smell of it. Like a desert.

Ann   My cocoa butter may / be?

Sophie   Well it's nice.

Then /

15

Hotel hallway. Lanzarote.

Ann   Already ate.

Sophie   How? Where? We're literally in the middle of . . .

Ann *smiles.*

Sophie   What . . .?

Ann   Don't, er. I. Well I did my 30 mins easy down the road. There's a drive-through on the roundabout.

Sophie   The McDonald's?! You went / to

Ann   Don't tell coach! I'm just sooo sick of pasta, innit.

Sophie   No, that's . . . Haaaa! *Fuck*, I'd kill for some McNuggets.

Ann   Babe, that was just my starter. Listen . . . Friday treat day.

Sophie   You get a burger then?

Ann   McChicken.

Sophie   Chips?

Ann   Yeah, obviously. Happy meal. No messing about.

Sophie   Ketchup?

Ann   Mayo.

Sophie   *Dirty.*

Ann   Fifteen grams of protein in a chicken burger I'll have you know.

Sophie   That right?

Ann   Yep. Works for Usain Bolt, works for me.

Sophie   Ha. Fair fucks.

Sophie *smiles. And /*

16

Hallway. Lanzarote.

Sophie   There are *two* Save the Last Dances?!

Ann   Apparently so.

Sophie *mimes vomiting.* Ann *laughs.*

Ann   Gotta do my coursework anyways.

Sophie   What is it?

Ann   Art. Just like annotating stuff.

Sophie   You do art?

Ann *nods.*

Sophie   Can I see?

Ann   Ha, nooope.

Sophie   Why not?

Ann   Coz . . .

Sophie   You can draw me if you want.

She poses. Ann *laughs.*

Sophie   I'm serious. It can be like, you know, *Titanic*.

Ann   What?

Sophie   The film.

Ann   Never seen it.

Sophie   You haven't seen *Titanic*?!

Ann *shakes her head. Beat.*

Ann   I can't draw people, you'll end up looking like a slug. Anyways, I've done the actual art I just need to like annotate. It's stupid.

Sophie   Well I was thinking of streaming the boxing if you wanna do it in front of that?

Ann *smiles. Beat, and /*

17

Playground. Lanzarote. Sophie *yanks her shoes off.*

Sophie   Come on! First one to / the

Ann   Hold on, gimme a . . . ouch! Little / prick!

Sophie   What?

Ann   Mosquito! / Little . . .

Sophie   Come on!

Sophie *swings up and on top of the bars.* Ann *struggles with her shoe.*

Sophie   Oooowwwooooooohhhhhh!

Ann   You / nutter!

Sophie   Oooooooowooooh, I'm on top of the worrrrrld! You can see the whole town. Come on, what are you doing?

Ann   How did you / get

Sophie   Up the side.

Ann   Is it strong enough?

Sophie   Are YOU strong / enough?

Ann   Shut upppp.

Sophie *pulls her top off and chucks it at* Ann.

Ann   Oi!

Ann *pulls hers off too. Chucks it back. Misses.*

Sophie   *Come on!*

Ann *climbs up to join her. She covers her chest.*

Ann   Hope no one comes over, whilst we're naked.

Sophie   We're not / *naked*

Ann   Woooaaah!!!

Sophie   *Yeah.*

Ann   Wow, is that Tenerife?! Morocco? Is that *Morocco*?!

Sophie   You can't see Morocco from / here

Ann   Well which way are we facing? East?

Sophie *slowly stands up.*

Ann   Careful . . .!!

Ann *tentatively stands too. They hold hands.*

Ann   Oh my gosh, ohhh my gosh. Ah. OK. OK.

She lets go of her hands. Raises them up.

Ann   Hahaaaaa! I feel. Like the queen. Of the universe.
Like I can do anything.

Ann *loses balance. Screams. Covers mouth.*

Sophie   Watch it!

They lower themselves. Sophie *swings down.*

Sophie   Right come on then, race you. You start that end,
I'll start here?

Ann   What are we doing?

Sophie   First one to the middle rung. The one, two . . . fifth
one in. Ready?

Ann   No, no wait! Standing start or it's not fair. *Wait . . .!*

She climbs down. Limbers up.

Ann   Alright. Alright . . .

Sophie   On your marks.

Ann   Set.

Both   Go!

They monkey-bar race. Collide in the middle. Sophie *wraps her legs around* Ann, *and they fall, scrambling, laughing, out of breath. They unpick themselves from each other, and* Ann *stands, holding out her hand sassily – victoriously.*

Sophie   Erm no, that was 100 per cent a draw.

Ann   *'Errrrrm, no'*, that's the middle, and we met here, / so

Sophie   Yeah but look, there's a bigger gap here, so that's actually the middle.

Ann   I dunno / man . . .

Sophie   *Look*! Bigger gap! If anything I pipped it.

Ann *carefully examines the gap. Frowns.*

Ann   Call it a draw.

Sophie *smiles. Beat.*

Ann   Do you reckon you're, er . . . competitive, Sophie?

Sophie   Fuck offfff.

Sophie *tries to cuff her, but* Ann *scrambles up. They sit. Swing legs.*

Ann   You started racing young right?

Sophie   Yeahhhh, I was like, nine.

Ann   *Nine*?!

Sophie   Yep. I was on the primary school lacrosse team then they realised I was 'better without the stick'.

Ann   OK, OK, skrrrrrrt! You had a *primary school lacrosse* team? *Daymm*. Or should I say: 'golly / gosh!'

Sophie   Shut uppppp. *Anyway*, they made me do mini marathon and turns out I was kinda quick, then Paul spotted me and / then

Ann   'The rest is history.'

Sophie *sticks her tongue out.*

Ann   *Nine years old?*

Sophie   Mmhmm. I'll be arthritic by thirty.

Ann   You should take cod liver oil.

Sophie   Euuugh!

Ann   No I'm serious, my mum swears by it.

Sophie   That is / *rank*.

Ann   Honestly!

Sophie   It's literally the liver of a cod. There are like proper supplements now. Haven't we moved past / fish liver

Ann   Do you see fish taking supplements for swimming?

Sophie   Yeah, / but

Ann   You see fish getting arthritis?

Sophie   I /

Ann   *Exactly*, trust me, Mum knows nothing about sports, yeah, but she knows her omegas.

Sophie   What does she do?

Ann   Care worker. Like old people.

Sophie   That's cool. My mum does like PR. Boring.

Ann   'PR.'

Sophie   Like companies and stuff. Like branding.

Ann   Yeah, I know what it is, I swear everyone works in 'PR'.

Sophie   We don't work in PR.

Ann   We don't work.

Sophie   Yeah, we do, we're athletes, duh.

Ann   It's not our job though.

Sophie   Well I get paid, don't I?

Ann   Yeah, but you're like a *big deal*, right? *Adidas*, man . . . it's *so cooool*.

Sophie *grins. Beat.*

Ann   Do you think I could . . . get, like, sponsored?

Sophie *shrugs. Nods.*

Ann   I'd probably have to lose like five seconds.

Sophie   Well, if you keep improving. Play your cards right.

Ann *imagines it for a moment.*

Ann   Still kind of PR though, isn't it? 'Personally Representing' Great Britain.

Sophie   Ha. 'Personally Representing Asics.'

Ann   *'Asics'*?! Arrrrre you kidding? If I get sponsorship it's gonna be *Nike* all the way, I'm not walking around in Asics when I could be wearing ticks.

Sophie *laughs.*

Ann   Imagine if I actually did though. Man I'd *love* to see Dad's face if I got paid! 'You can't eat your lap times Ann.' 'Your body is not a sustainable career choice.' He wants me to come live with him in Lagos. Thinks I'm gonna screw my exams and become a / hobo

Sophie   But you're *such* a geek.

Ann   Yeah, but he reckons anything below A-star is a ticket to being a drug addict or something. Like B stands for brothel.

Sophie   I'm just trying not to fail. Home straight. C stands for 'Couldn't give a fuck'.

Ann   Tell that to Dad and he'd lose his *mind*.

Sophie   Tell it to him when we've got Olympic golds and see what he says then.

Ann *grins. Beat. They let themselves imagine it.*

Ann   Do you reckon you could break two minutes?

Beat. Sophie *nods, suddenly serious.*

Sophie   It's all about peaking at the right . . . I'm on track. Like, I'm still under 20s, right. When I finish sixth form I'll have more time to train. If I can push up to top five seniors . . . We've like, got a plan. I mean it's steps, right: Nationals, Euros, Worlds . . .

Beat. Ann *nods, mesmerised.*

Sophie   Did you watch London 2012?

Ann   Er, yeah . . . like on TV.

Sophie   Yeah, I mean me too, Mum balloted for literally everything, didn't get one ticket. But you know the bid song?

Ann *shakes her head.*

Sophie   No, you do. You *do*, it's like, it's famous, it's like 'What have you done today, to make you feeeel prrou / uuud'

Ann   Ohhhh *that*, / yeah!

Sophie   Exactly!

Ann   *That song*! I love that / song!

Sophie   Yeah, it was *everywhere* here. And that first year I did the mini marathon was the year of the Olympics right, and I remember them playing it while I was running up the Mall, like the last stretch, by Buckingham Palace, and I literally felt like I was *levitating*, gonna take / off

Ann   'It's never too late to tryyyy / yyyyy'

Sophie   I still listen to it before every race.

Ann   What? Seriously?!

Sophie   Yeah. I got like a little playlist. 'Proud.' Kanye West. Aretha Franklin, / er

Ann   That is some mixed kebab of a / playlist

Sophie   Elton John . . . / Sean Paul . . .

Ann   You listen to *Elton John* before a race?!

Sophie   Yeah, it makes me happy I dunno, reminds me of / my

Ann   *Elton John?!* Nah, that is / *funny*

Sophie   Fuck off, what's wrong with Elton / John?

Ann   No, well, sure, I mean . . . it clearly works, so.

Sophie *laughs. Shrugs. Beat.*

Ann   D'you actually think I could get sponsored?

Sophie   Paul knows talent when he sees it.

Ann   Like you.

Sophie   Like all of us. Like where did you come at English Schools?

Ann   You know where I came. Like how you knew exactly how tall I was in camp check-ins before I did. Like how I know pretty much the entire history of your athletics career and every other middle-distance girl in the group.

Sophie *smiles.*

Sophie   You came fourth. Up with Iz Baxter. 2.08.2. Your first national competition. You're really fucking good.

Ann *smiles. Beat. They look at the view.*

Sophie   Imagine if they were actually made of gold. You'd have to be an Olympic weight-lifter just to wear it.

Ann *laughs. She stands. Raises her arms.*

Ann   'It's never too late to tryyyyyyyyyy, what have / you'

She loses her balance, shrieks.

Sophie   Watch it, you mentalist!

Ann *balances.* Beat. Sophie *watches her.*

Sophie   Are your parents divorced then?

Ann   Huh?

Sophie   You said your dad lives in Lagos.

Ann   Oh. No. Ha no. They're solid. Reckon Mum'll move over when me and Dean finish school. Dad . . . like they came to England coz, England, but he never . . . like London never really felt like home. It's different for Mum, she's got family, church and like she did college here, so . . . Yeah.

Sophie   That is *proper* long distance.

Ann   They love a video chat.

Sophie *smiles.*

Sophie   My dad lives in Harrogate.

Ann   I didn't know you had a dad.

Sophie   Everyone's got a dad.

Ann   Ha. Touché.

Beat. Ann *curls her arms through the warm air.*

Sophie   I reckon Karl fancies you, you know. He was staring at you the whole of circuits.

Ann   *Karl?* Ha. No he doesn't. Anyways, I got a boyfriend, so.

Sophie   Do you?

Ann   Yep. Simon.

Sophie   From school?

Ann   Church.

Sophie   How long?

Ann   Like . . . eleven weeks?

Sophie   'Simon from church.'

Ann *grins, embarrassed. Beat.*

Sophie   Have you noticed how big and flat Karl's face is? Flat and pale. Like the cliffs of Dover.

Ann *laughs.*

Sophie   Seriously, he should get a handicap, there's nothing aerodynamic about that. Miracle he can walk, let alone run.

Ann   Haaaa. And he *totally* doesn't know how to talk to girls.

Sophie   Well yeah, classic runner virgin.

Sophie *stands up. They balance.*

Ann   I'm a runner virgin.

Sophie   Yeah but you don't pretend you're not.

Beat.

Ann   At dinner Rob was saying how he'd had a threesome.

Sophie   Baaahaa, SUCH BOLLOCKS!

Ann   Says he did.

Sophie   Little Rob?! He can't even wobble board, imagine him trying to juggle *two* . . .

They cackle, struggling to keep balance, but /

Wait!! Shh! What was that?!

They freeze. A torch light. They scramble down.

Ann   Is it coach?!

Sophie   Shit. Get / down!

Ann   Do you think he / saw

Sophie   Fuck fuck / fuck!

Ann   He's gonna kill us!

Sophie   He might not have / seen

Ann   He literally shone it right at / us!

Sophie   If we run we might be able to sneak in around the . . . Shit, is he coming over?!

Ann   Oh my gossssshhhh!

Ann can't find her top. Sophie *laughs.*

Ann   Shhhh!

Sophie   You shhhhhh!

The girls hide, desperately trying not to laugh.

Get lower! Crouch in front of me! He's gonna see!

Ann   It's not my fault you're basically glow in the dark!

Sophie *laughs.* Ann *claps a hand over her mouth. They suppress giggles. Then hold their breath, as the torch passes over them and disappears. Coast finally clear, they fall about laughing.*

Sophie   Oh my godddd, you were shitting yourself!

Ann   No I wasn't.

Sophie   You were, you were shaking!

Ann   I was laughing coz you farted!

Sophie   No I didn't!

Ann   You did!

Sophie   No / I

Ann   You telling me that was a phantom fart, some ghost / fart

Sophie   Haaa, you were *so* scared.

Ann   Well, it's OK for you, you're his golden gal.

Sophie   Quick, come on, before he checks our rooms.

Sophie *throws* Ann's *top at her.* Ann *pulls it on wrong.* Sophie *helps. Beat.*

Sophie   I'm gonna miss you back home.

Ann   I'm *literally* gonna see you in training.

Sophie   Yeah, but like . . .

Ann   Yeah.

Ann *smiles. Beat.*

Ann   Do you sometimes feel like coach looks at you with like X-Ray vision? Like he can see everything?

Sophie   I mean that's his job. 'Refining our machines.'

Ann   Ha. 'Oiling our motors.'

Sophie   'Lubricating our . . . / cogs'

Ann   Ewwwhh!

Sophie   Ha. No, but seriously. He knows his shit. And if he thinks you're good . . . You're good.

Ann *swallows, nods, then /*

MOVEMENT

Music plays. Maybe 'Proud'. They lace their shoes . . . and train. Hard. It's euphoric. Dynamic. A dance, that builds and builds . . . a glorious celebration of what the body can do . . . then /

18

BANG! Stadium. Trackside.

Ann   YES, YOU *QUEEN*! Come / here!

Sophie   No, I might puke on / you

Ann   You nailed it!

Sophie   It's only southern / champs

Ann   Don't care. You absolutely *slapped* it, you were on fire! Straight to the final, babyyyy!

Sophie   See you there, yeah?

Ann makes a face.

Sophie   No no, none of that. How long 'til your heat?

Ann   Ten / minutes

Sophie   How you feeling . . .?

Ann opens her mouth, but Sophie *covers it. Grabs her. Bounces her around.*

Sophie   Shutthefuckup . . . Shutthefuckup . . . Shutthefuck / up

Ann   Your armpits / *reek*

Sophie   Shutthefuckup.

They both laugh . . . then BANG! /

19

Surrey Hills. Mid-run. Hot. Breathless.

Ann   Woooooa / aaah!

Sophie   We can't / *stop*

Ann   Where are we? I mean / what

Sophie   'Surrey Hills, Area of Outstanding / Natural Beauty.'

Ann   It's *sooo / beautiful*!

Sophie   Ha, does what it says on the / tin

Ann   This is like legit English countryside, like when people think of England, this is / what they

Sophie   Look, we can't stop, our heart rates will / drop

Ann   I do my steadies around the *soccer pitch*.

Sophie   What? Like thirty times around?!

Ann   Mum doesn't like me running on the street at night.

Sophie   Just get up early before school, that's what I / do

Ann   How early?

Sophie   Like five forty-five?

Ann *freezes*. Sophie *laughs*.

Ann   That is absolutely disgusting. That's mental. That is / absolutely

Sophie   Well come sleep over next weekend and we can do our Sunday long run together? I'll get Mum to drive us to Leith Hill, now *that's* / beautiful

Ann   Can't. Church.

Sophie   Ohhh yeah . . . Alright, come on. *Come on* or we'll seize up. The next mile's up, but then there's this *amazing* downhill where it's like your legs are spinning / under you

Ann   Sweeeeeeeeeet . . .

And /

20

Track stands. UK Junior Champs. Start guns. Crowd.

Ann   *Together*?! Marmite and jam . . . to / gether

Sophie   Yep.

Ann   Nah, that is / *weird*

Sophie   It's salt and sweet.

Ann   Yeah, / but

Sophie   Think about it.

Ann   I am. And it's / disgusting

Sophie   Perfect pre-race snack. Complex carbs, sugar, salt.

Ann   . . . but it's disgusting.

Sophie   You have sweet and salty popcorn.

Ann   *I* don't.

Sophie   OK but *people* do.

Ann   *That's* your good luck routine? Marmite, jam and Elton John?

Sophie   I told you not to / ask!

Ann   I am dead, I am / *dead!*

Sophie   I told you it was silly!!! Well, *you* always have that orange rice.

Ann   Jollof?

Sophie   Yeah.

Ann   But that's a legitimately normal meal! That's *food*! That's an actual *meal*! Right so, so what if you're out of Marmite?

Sophie   That's impossible coz I prep the day before. Look, I know it's mad, but it's like superstition, right?

Ann   Like that thing you do with your back?

Sophie   What thing?

Ann *mimics* Sophie *on the start line.*

Sophie   I don't do that!

Ann   Yesss you do. You look like a shark that's smelled blood.

Sophie *laughs. She likes that.*

Sophie   What about this then . . .

Sophie *sits up straight and mimes kissing a cross, looking up, then down. She jiggles her shoulders, pumping herself up.* Ann *can't help but smile.* Sophie *turns the jiggle into a shimmy.* Ann *cuffs her. A start gun goes: BANG! – making them jump and look out at the track.*

Ann   Wait, who's / this?!

Sophie   Under 17s.

Ann   *YES*, ROB! GO ON / ROBBIE!

Sophie   COME ON, ROBBBB / STAAA!

Ann   YES, ROBBIIIE! *You got thissss!*

Sophie   Come on mate . . . Come / on . . .

Ann   Nah, he's dropped / the

Sophie   Come on, Robbbbbbieeee . . .

They watch them finish. Beat.

Ann   How long we got?

Sophie   Still ages.

Ann *squirms and rubs her belly.*

Ann   Right. I'm gonna do more revision. Don't talk to me.

Sophie   Borrrrrrring.

Ann   Haven't you got / to

Sophie   Yeahhhh, but it's biology. *Bleeeeugh.*

Sophie *stretches.*

Sophie   I'm thirsty.

Ann   Probably that nasty Marmite and /

Sophie *shoves her, and moves off and then /*

MOVEMENT

Pre-race routines, pumping themselves up . . . then: BANG! A race. And BANG! Another. BANG! Ann gaining confidence with every start, and /

21

Track.

Ann   Not great.

Sophie   By which you mean . . . top marks.

Ann   Ha, no. Dad's proper pissed. I'm gonna drop the art, and retake the maths / and

Sophie   I'm sure you did *fine*. Come on. Strides.

And /

MOVEMENT

Training. Euphoric. Charged. Until /

22

Gym. Stretching.

Ann   Well it serves her right, innit. What . . .? It does.

Sophie   Do you really think she did it on purpose?

Ann   She had a tonne of THG in her piss!

Sophie   It said 'traces of'.

Ann   It wasn't an *accident*, you don't *accidentally* eat steroids.

Sophie   I dunno, I just, like, what's the point?

Ann   Twenty-grand prize money?

Sophie   Yeah but like even if you did get away with it, which obviously you won't, you'd know it wasn't, like, *real*.

Ann   Well, bumps you into top five, doesn't it? Nice spot to end the season.

Sophie *frowns*.

Ann   What?! She cheated. You didn't. She's out, you're in. Fair's fair. Bumps me up the ranks too. *What . . .?* It's true!

Sophie   No, yeah, no I agree with *that*, obviously, it just, it freaks me out, like what if . . . Like how do you know that those chemicals aren't just like, in something you eat?

Ann   There's a list on the IAAF website.

Sophie   Yeah, but I don't know what's in my lunch, do I?

Ann   Oh actually there *is* Stanozolol in the Tesco BLT.

Sophie   What?! Are / you

Ann   Obviously not, / you tool!

Sophie   Oh! Ha!

And /

MOVEMENT

They train. Hard. Pushing. And /

23

Gym. Both exhausted.

Sophie   This is the grind time. When we get strong.

Ann   Yeah. Yep. It's just the dark, man. Morning. Evening. Like at least you get to run in daylight, I'm so jealous, I wish I was done with school.

Sophie   You love ittt. Whenever I message you, 'oh, just doing my coursework'.

Ann *makes a face.*

Sophie   It'll whizz by. Resits Jan. Indoors Feb. Summer season prep. Exams, blah, done by July in time for the big comps.

And /

MOVEMENT

They train. Hard. Tired. Pushing. And /

24

Trackside. Sophie *suddenly small.*

Sophie   Breast cancer.

Ann   What?!

Sophie   Mum had a lump / and

Ann   What / ?

Sophie   The biopsy came back and it's breast cancer.

Ann   I . . . Come here.

Sophie   We have to warm up.

Ann   Come here.

Ann *hugs her.* Sophie *leans in. Starts to shake.*

Ann   Hey hey hey. I got you.

Sophie *rests her head on* Ann's *chest and exhales. She holds on tight . . . Before pushing into /*

MOVEMENT

Training. No other thoughts, but /

25

Gym.

Sophie   Well, it's Dad's turn so it's Harrogate. Traditional. Like stockings, walk, food. You?

Ann   What do you think . . .?

Sophie   Church?

Ann *grins, nods, and /*

26

Sophie*'s bedroom. On the floor.* Sophie *laughing.*

Ann   Shhhhhhh! Carol's sleeping!

Sophie   It's fine, her bedroom's miles away. She's probably drunk anyway.

Ann   OK, so, what, she just told you about them?!

Sophie   Yeah, cupboard above the sink.

Ann   Like they're for you?

Sophie   Well, *she's* not gonna use them, is she, she's all menopausal.

Ann   So?

Sophie   So her periods have stopped so she can't get pregnant, duh.

Ann   *Oh.* Can you not get pregnant if you don't get your period?

Sophie   Er, no.

Ann   I don't get them.

Sophie   Me neither. Like literally once in a blue moon. The medic says it's normal. Too much training, stops your cycles.

Ann   Right. OK so wait, so she leaves them in the bathroom / . . .

Sophie   Yeah. Yeah, *basically* like ages ago she did this awkward thing, literally when I was like thirteen, and she was like 'they're in there if you need them, wink wink', I was like 'no really, Mum, I don't need condoms', and she was like 'Oooookay, wink wink . . . but, er, just so you know', and I was like 'no seriously, Mum, I've literally only got to first base and it barely even counts coz it was pizza-face Pete'.

Ann   Who's pizza-face Pete?!

Sophie   Some guy in my year. Weedy and spotty with these little patches of bumfluff.

Ann   Wow, sounds like a *riiiide*.

Sophie   Beggars can't be choosers, bae.

Ann   Shut uppp, you were obviously super popular at school.

Sophie   Not really.

Ann   Really?

Sophie   What?

Ann   No, it's just you're like . . .

Sophie   What?

Ann   What?

Sophie   Like what?

Ann   Like, fit. Aren't you?

Sophie   Am I?

Ann   Come on, Soph, you could get *annny* guy you liked.

Sophie Er, well firstly, no. And secondly, boys are annoying.

Ann *laughs.*

Ann But you've . . . I mean have you . . .

Sophie Yeah, but just, like, once. It's not . . . I mean, it was fine, but it wasn't like some amazing . . . thing.

Beat.

Ann The idea of my mum talking about condoms makes me high key *stressed*. Like we just pretend that stuff doesn't exist.

Sophie But you've done sex-ed at school right?

Ann Yeah, wrap the banana, don't get pregnant, don't get crabs, bye bye.

Sophie *laughs. Beat. She watches* Ann *carefully.*

Sophie Are you and Simon . . .?

Ann No!

Sophie But do you want to?

Ann Mum would kill me.

Sophie But do you *want* to?

Beat. Ann *shrugs. Nods. Shrugs. Then she laughs.*

Ann You know how we went to the *Lion King* for Si's birthday with his parents?

Sophie Yeah . . .

Ann Yeah, right, yeah, well in the middle of it I reached over for the Fanta, right, but I grabbed his, like his you know, by mistake? And, he, um . . . oh my / gosh

Sophie What?

Ann He got a . . . like / a . . .

Sophie A boner?!

Ann *covers her face*. Sophie *laughs*.

Sophie   *What*?! Oh my goddd, how did you not tell me about / this?!

Ann   And then I wanted to move my hand right, but it felt even more awkward, so I just kind of . . . left it there and . . .

Sophie *is hysterical now*.

Everyone got up in the interval and he just had to sit there 'til it . . . you know. I think maybe he thought I wanted to jerk him off to Simba or / something

Sophie   Hahaa! Aaaahhh senvntyaaa / aaaa

Ann   No, no shut / uppppp

Sophie   Baaabbbabbagiiiissiibaa / awwbaaaa

Ann   Shhhhhh! Carol!

They stifle their laughter.

Sophie   OK, right then, so verdict is it all works, and he wants to?

Ann   Nahh. I don't know. I mean I don't even think I . . . Anyways his dad's a pastor. Super religious. More than Mum. Like fully no sex before marriage kinda thing.

Sophie   Well, would you marry him?

Ann *shrugs. Nods.*

Sophie   Really?!

Ann   Yeah, I mean not right now / obviously

Sophie   No but like . . . in the future?

Ann *nods, smiles, embarrassed.*

Sophie   Oooooooohhh!

Ann   Stop ittt!

Sophie   Do you love him? Oh my God you / do!

Ann   Well, yeah, of course / I do

Sophie   Dya wanna have babies with him?

Ann   I. Yeah, I mean one day, / I

Sophie   Oh my God do you actually?!

Ann   Yeah! What?

Sophie   No, I just didn't . . . How do you know?

Ann   I just do.

Sophie   How many?

Ann   Two boys, two girls.

Sophie   *Four?!*

Ann   I want a big / family

Sophie   How are you gonna run with four babies?!

Ann   I dunno. Sling 'em on. Two on the back, two on the front. Weight training, innit.

Sophie *laughs.*

Ann   Anyway I'm not talking about *now*. I mean after. You know, Olympics or two, get my medals, do my time. Then . . . get fat, buy a big house and have a load of kids.

Sophie   You could never get / fat

Ann   How many do you want?

Sophie   Um . . . I dunno. My mum's always like 'don't dooo itttt'.

Ann   Ever?

Sophie   Well I was a 'mistake', so.

Ann   Not 'mistake'. 'Unplanned.'

Sophie *shrugs.*

Sophie   Oh my God, imagine Paul's face if one of us got preggo. He'd freak. He's literally a-sexual.

Ann   When he was trying to do that chat at camp, you know after Lyds and Sean hooked up, when he was all 'Now obviously, er, er, it's not my business what goes on between, er / . . .'

Sophie   I bet he's never even done it. Bet he can't. Like, I bet it's all smooth down there. Like an action man.

Ann *makes a face*. Sophie *laughs*. *Beat*.

Sophie   Well, no mistakes if we don't get periods right? That and you being a massive virgin.

Ann   Hey, Mother Mary did it. Never say never.

Beat. Sophie *looks at* Ann. Ann *looks back*.

Sophie   Do you actually / believe

Ann   No! *Obviously / not!*

Sophie   Well I dunno! I was just trying to be . . . you said you believed in rebirth. Spirits. The Holy / Trinity

Ann   Yeah but it's not *literal*!

Beat.

Sophie   I kind of like not having to think about them you know.

Ann   What?

Sophie   Periods. Like when I do get them, like when I used to, I felt *awful*, like it's horrible, right? And five days a month feeling crap, so every year that's what . . . fifty / days

Ann   Sixty / days

Sophie   Yeah. Sixty crap training days a year. Not worth it.

Ann *shakes her head*.

Sophie   Like, I just want to run. That's all I really want.

Ann   Me too.

Beat. Then /

27

Track car park. Cold. Ann *catching* Sophie *up.*

Ann   That looked nasty.

Sophie   It's normal.

Ann   I've never seen him shout like that.

Sophie   Well, normal for if I'm crap.

Ann   You weren't / crap

Sophie   He just wants me to do my best. Pushes me that's all.

Ann   We all have off / days

Sophie   It's not a big deal. Paul's right. Head wasn't in the game.

Ann   But I mean it's just training.

Sophie   It's never just training.

Ann   We've got weeks 'til the / indoor champs

Sophie   Look, it's not a big deal, OK? I had a slow one. Come on.

Ann   Come on where? Where's / Carol?

Sophie   Bus stop. Mum's got hospital.

Ann *nods. And follows her into /*

MOVEMENT

Training. Hard. Then /

28

Stadium. Trackside. Ann *radiates confidence.*

Sophie   Where did you go?! I . . . congratu-fucking-lations! That / was

Ann   Thanks / !

Sophie   Incredible! Where did that . . . Come here! You were on fire! That was . . . you must've knocked like three seconds off?!

Ann   Yeah! I / Yeah!

Sophie   Seriously, you were doing *negative splits*, plenty more in the tank! Paul was loosing his shit, did you hear him? 'Nought to a hundred, look at her go!' 'What a PB!' What happened to holding back in the heats?!

Ann   Ha, I / dunno

Sophie   Literally, where did that come from?!

Ann *shrugs, grins, overwhelmed.*

Ann   I had to do some photo thing.

Sophie   Yeah?!

Ann   *Athletics Weekly*? I hope they airbrush it. I probably looked like I was about to die.

Sophie   Ha. Well . . . I'll . . . I'll see you in the final then?

Ann *nods. Smiles.*

Ann   Gonna warm down before I stiffen up.

Sophie *watches* Ann *go, her eyes filled with something: Pride? Fear? And so . . .*

MOVEMENT

Training, competition creeping in now.

29

Both bend. Sophie *slaps* Ann *on the back.*

Sophie   Nice work.

And /

MOVEMENT

They train harder: Sophie *just ahead, and /*

30

They bend, exhausted.

Sophie   Jesu / s.

Ann   Yep.

Breathe, and /

MOVEMENT

They train: Ann *close now, and /*

31

Mid-session. Out of breath.

Sophie   Owh / fuck

Ann   Sorry. / Sorry

Sophie   It's OK.

Ann   Did I spike your heel? Are you / OK?

Sophie   It's fine.

And /

MOVEMENT

Training: Ann *nearly catching* Sophie, *and /*

32

They bend.

Ann   Good / job

Sophie   You too.

They stand, breathe, take marks again, and /

MOVEMENT

BANG! They race. Elbow to elbow . . . fierce, charged, until they come to a 'stop' at exactly the same time. They bend. Hands on backs. They move apart, catching breath. Quiet, until /

33

Track.

Ann   Well Saucony are offering more money.

Sophie   But / . . .?

Ann   But I'm going for Nike, obviously.

Sophie   *Whyyy* do you love Nike so much?

Ann   Coz they're COOL.

Sophie   So have you signed the thing, or . . .

Ann   Coach is looking over the paperwork. Mum's all stressed. Worried I'm selling my soul.

Sophie   Screw your soul, babe, you're *sponsored*.

Ann   Man, it's like . . . *proper cash*. Like a salary. I'm gonna save and put a deposit down on Mum's place. Go on holiday! Dean's trying to get me to buy flat-screen, haaa.

Sophie *smiles, and /*

34

Sophie*'s bedroom. Cozy.* Ann *miming a mic;* Sophie *pretending to be out of breath.*

Sophie   Um, yeah, well, look I just went out there and tried my best, and yeah . . . I felt strong. I'm chuffed.

Ann   Mm. Mmmm . . . and it was pretty close, huh?

Sophie   Well, there were some amazing performances, we all ran a good race, any of us could've pushed through / but

Ann *breaks character, laughs.*

Sophie   What?

Ann   Nah, it's just funny right, how you have to be all like 'ah it was so close', but like . . . I'd just say it how it is, like 'yeah, I killed it, I'm the fastest'.

Sophie   You can't say *that*!

Ann   Why not?

Sophie   Well, you have to sound modest. Humble. People will think you're an arrogant prick.

Ann   Muhammed Ali did it. 'I'm the world's greatest, I'm the greatest.'

Sophie   Yeah, well, *we* can't say that.

Ann   LeBron James: 'Ask me to play; I'll play!' You won coz I were fastest, right? You got gold. You're the G.O.A.T.

Sophie   Well, it's imaginary, isn't it, it's not a / real

Ann   Yeah and we *imagined* you won.

Sophie   Yeah / but . . .

Ann   Alright my turn.

Sophie   OK. What did you get?

Ann   Gold, *obviously*.

Sophie   OK . . .

Ann *clears her throat, mimes the mic, and* /

35

Changing rooms.

Sophie   What is it? Just tell me!

Ann   It doesn't matter.

Sophie   If it doesn't matter, just tell me! Why are you being . . . Is it thrush?!

Ann   *No.*

Sophie   Is it . . . It's not something . . . you know . . . is it?

Ann   What?

Sophie   You're not, like it's not something like . . . dodgy?

Ann   No! It's . . . It *doesn't / matter*

Sophie   I'm suuuuper confused.

Ann   It's. Ah! It's hair removal cream, OK?! I get hair on my top lip and you could see it in the sponsorship shoot thing and the guys took the piss, so I thought I'd . . .

Sophie   Oh. / *Ohhhh!*

Ann   Yeah.

Sophie   Everyone has hair there!

Ann   Yeah, but you can *see* mine. Mine's dark.

Sophie   I can't see / any

Ann   Yeah, that's coz I Veeted it off, didn't I?!

Sophie *starts laughing.*

Ann   It's not funny!

Sophie   Sorry.

Ann   It's nasty. It smells like fish. I left it in the bathroom one time and Mum nearly used it as toothpaste by mistake.

Sophie *laughs harder.*

Sophie   Bald gums.

Ann   It's not funny!

Sophie   Yes it is!

Ann   Imagine that fishy chemical stuff in your mouth!

Sophie *laughs harder.* Ann *can't help join in, and /*

36

Gym. Doing plank.

Sophie   But like, do you talk to Him like he's a mate, or . . .

Ann   Who says it's a Him?

Sophie   OK, / but

Ann   No, I kind of . . . put good vibes out.

Sophie   Like before running?

Ann   Yeah. And other stuff. Thirty seconds to go.

Sophie *nods. They're starting to shake now.*

Sophie   Do you think it makes you go faster?

Ann   Soph . . .

Sophie   Like, I mean, do you think it works?

Ann   Can we not do this again?

Sophie   I just / meant

Ann   It's not a transactional thing. It's not like . . . magic fairy dust.

Sophie   No but . . . you believe in it?

Ann *looks at the time. Relaxes.* Sophie *copies.*

Ann   I'm still working it out. Finding my way of . . . Like I think for me it's not about the actual . . . It's the feeling. When I talk to God or whatever it's more like checking in with a bit of *me*. Like centring. Like. Like you know when you're on the blocks, OK, and the whole world kind of contracts? And you're inside yourself for a second. Just you and your brain. It's like that. When I pray I'm not asking for stuff, it's not a negotiation.

Beat.

Sophie   Sorry, no it's just I. It's just I started doing it a bit.

Ann   Praying?

Sophie *nods. She stretches. Beat.*

Sophie   Do you believe in heaven?

Ann *watches* Sophie. *Nods. Beat.*

Ann   How is Carol?

Sophie   Er, yeah . . . she's alright. She's fucking hard you know.

Ann   No guessing where you get it from.

Sophie *smiles.*

Sophie   Paul told me that fifty per cent of our power is psychological. Twenty-five per cent base level. Twenty-five per cent training. Fifty per cent mind.

Ann   And five per cent those weird energy drinks you chug.

Sophie   I'm being serious.

Ann *smiles. Beat.*

Ann   'If you had faith even as small as a mustard seed, you could say to this mountain, "Move from here to there," and it would move. Nothing would be impossible.'

Sophie   Who said that?

Ann   Jesus.

Sophie *nods sincerely. Beat.* Ann *laughs.*

Sophie   What?

Ann   No, it's just your face! *It's not that deep.*

Sophie'*s frown turns into a smile, but /*

37

Gym.

Sophie   AKA chubby. Whenever anyone says 'strong', it means chubby. It's like when Mum says I'm glowing, it's basically shorthand for 'are you pregnant'?

Ann *chuckles.*

Sophie   I just think if they were a / bit lighter

Ann   Don't go there, it's stupid. They're literally made of / muscle

Sophie   I'm just / saying

Ann   Feel them.

Sophie   Stop it.

Ann   Feel them! / They're

Sophie   Ouch! You're pinching my / fat

Ann   Muscle. Pure muscle. If it was fat it wouldn't hurt. See?

Sophie   No, see? Bum fat!

Ann It's your glute!

Sophie Bum.

Ann Glute.

Sophie I'm just saying don't you ever wish that you were a bit lighter, you know like those Eastern European girls?

Ann Not at all.

Sophie Never?

Ann No. No, coz that's not me. I'm strong. My job is to be fast. If I was supposed to be a ballerina or something, I'd be screwed but . . . what?

Sophie No, sorry, it's just the idea of you being a ballerina.

Ann Excuse me. I can be incredibly graceful.

Ann *does ballet.* Sophie *laughs. Shakes her bum.*

Sophie Yeah. Good. That's it. Own it. *Own it.*

Ann *slaps* Sophie's *bum. She laughs, but /*

38

Track.

Ann Haven't you already jogged down?

Sophie Just doing a couple more / laps

Ann Coach said we should save ourselves for / Nationals

Sophie I just want to stretch out my / legs

Ann But /

Sophie Paul says it's fine. It's just a jog. What?

Ann I . . . Nothing.

And /

39

Track.

Ann   A new set of what?

Sophie   A pair.

Ann   Of what?

Sophie   *Tits*!

Ann   Oh!

Sophie   Like they had to take them off /

Ann   Oh, / *right*.

Sophie   So she's having plastic surgery. And she thought, fuck it, I might as well go up to a DD.

Ann   Wow. Go Carol. DD. That's like . . . *Boobs*. So, it's like completely gone?

Sophie   Her tit?

Ann   No! The cancer you / plum

Sophie   Oh, ha, yeah yeah. Pretty much, like she'll have to still keep having checks and stuff, but yeah, no more chemo, / so

Ann   That's amazing!

Sophie   Yeah!

Beat.

Ann   Is it bad that I'm kinda jealous?

Sophie   What?

Ann   *DD*, I mean . . .

Sophie   Ann, that's . . .

Ann   Sorry /

Sophie   Really, like really / disrespectful

Ann   Sorry, sorry.

Beat.

Sophie   *I'm joking.*

Ann   Oh right / haa!

Sophie   I'm fuming. I want a boob job. Imagine having *DD*?!

Ann   Imagine a B, hun.

Sophie *laughs.*

Sophie   They'd slow us down.

Ann   Yeah, yeah exactly.

Beat.

You got boobs.

Sophie   Nah, it's an illusion. They're just pecs with nipples on.

Ann *snorts.*

Sophie   Seriously, feel.

Ann   No!

Sophie   Seriously though, when I tense, feel, seriously, it's / just

Ann   Soph, I'm not feeling your / boob!

Sophie   I'm just proving / my

Ann   Soph!

Sophie *grabs her hand.*

Ann   Haaa! No!

Ann *scrunches up her face.* Sophie *reaches up to* Ann's *forehead and smooths her frown line away.*

Ann   What?

Sophie   You'll get old-man wrinkles. Don't wanna be flat chested *and* wrinkly.

Ann *goes to hit her.* Sophie *hits back.* Ann *grabs* Sophie's *hand, pulling her into a wrestle.*

Ann   Oh my God no! Nooo!

They end up standing close, breathing heavily, a tension between them. Beat. Then Ann *shifts back . . . and /*

40

Gym. Stretching.

Sophie   Didn't think it was a plus one kinda thing.

Ann   I can't just tell him to go home. He's coming all the way to Glasgow.

Sophie   Where's he staying?

Ann   Some hotel.

Sophie   On the Nikey tab?

Ann   Nah, I offered, but . . . he wouldn't let me.

Sophie   That's quite sweet. Slash hyper-masculine.

Beat.

Does it not add pressure? Like him travelling all the way here. Buying tickets to the dinner . . .?

Beat.

I probably won't even go. Those parties are dry.

Ann   Don't you wanna celebrate?

Sophie   Well, I don't know what I'll be celebrating yet.

Ann   'Gotta think win.'

Sophie *stares back. Beat.*

Sophie   I'll see how I feel on Sunday. I don't wanna jinx it.

Ann   That long-jumper's gonna be there.

Sophie   I DON'T FANCY MATTHIAS HALT.

Ann   YES YOU DO.

Sophie   I don't. I really don't.

Ann *dances around like 'suuuuuure'.* Sophie *watches her, a smile creeping in.*

I don't. I . . .

Sophie *keeps watching* Ann *spin and spin . . .*

MOVEMENT

And they're training . . . Ann *pulling ahead, and /*

41

Trackside.

Sophie   How are you feeling about it?

Ann   What?

Sophie   'What?' The Euros!

Ann   Yeah! I mean it's sick! Always wanted to go to Poland.

Sophie *laughs.*

Ann   What?

Sophie   I asked you how you were feeling about the Euros / and

Ann   Well I / don't know

Sophie   You're talking about sight-seeing. It's the biggest race you've / ever

Ann   Yeah / I

Sophie   You've just been selected / for the

Ann   Yeah, I know. I mean, yeah! It's exciting. Just gotta focus. Keep my head down.

Sophie   Well now you sound like a magazine interview.

Ann   Coach just said 'head down, focus, keep doing what you're doing'. I mean yeah, it's . . . a lot, like if I think about it I . . . I dunno, I mean how are you feeling about it?

Sophie   Yeah, cool. Never been to Warsaw. Gonna book a bus tour.

Ann   Fuck you, man.

Sophie *chuckles. Then she frowns, stares.*

Ann   What?

Sophie   You swore.

Ann   So.

Sophie   You never swear.

Ann   Yeah I do. Sometimes.

Sophie *raises her eyebrows. Grins. Then /*

42

Hallway.

Ann   Did you eat lunch?

Sophie *nods.*

Ann   When?

Sophie   In my room.

Ann   How?

Sophie   Room service.

Ann   Why? That's such a waste of . . .

Sophie *shrugs*.

Ann   Did you actually?

Sophie   Yes, none of your business, why does it matter?

Ann   Soph, you can't survive off those rank protein shakes. We're supposed to eat the canteen / stuff

Sophie   Why are you pushing this?

Ann   You need to eat / properly

Sophie   It's none of your business.

Ann   OK. I'm just . . . OK.

And /

MOVEMENT

Pre-race routine. Both nervous. Start positions, and . . . BANG!

They race. Ann *is flying.* Sophie *straining.* Ann *finishes. Then* Sophie. *They bend to catch their breath.* Ann *looks up at her clock, eyes alight.* Sophie *glances at hers, then turns away, and /*

43

Stadium car park. Sophie *walking off.*

Sophie   It was embarrassing.

Ann   Come on / Soph

Sophie   I died. I flopped it.

Ann   Where are you going? I thought we were gonna get / lunch

Sophie   Don't feel like it. Argh! *I know I can break two. I know I can. Fucksake. What's wrong with / me*

Ann   'Shutthefuckup, shutthefuck / up'

Sophie   Not helpful.

Ann   Look, you gotta take the highs with the . . . You can't win them all. You just had a / bad

Sophie   You sound like some self-help / book

Ann   Sorry /

Sophie   Cliché bollocks for people who can't get out of bed. I paced it wrong. I got lactic. You fucking slaughtered me. I got knocked out. I'm allowed to be annoyed.

Then /

44

Ann's *room. Hotel.*

Ann   *What?* I don't wanna watch Polish TV while everyone farts nervously and pretends they're friends, is that OK with you?

Sophie   You can do whatever you want.

Ann   Thank you.

Sophie   I just think it's a bit irresponsible.

Ann   Irresponsi / ble?

Sophie   Like it's the most important race you've ever done. You're into the final of the *Euros.* You've got possibly the best, biggest chance in your / life

Ann   Yes, I know / that

Sophie   And you're willing to fuck it up over some guy.

Ann   Si's here to support me. And he's not 'some guy', he's / my

Sophie   What you gonna do tonight then?

Ann   I dunno. Go get a pizza or something. Have an early night.

Sophie   Does the board know, does Paul know he's staying here?

Ann   Is it their business?! What's going on?

Sophie   Don't his parents mind?

Ann   Look we . . . Soph, we've shared a bed before. Like we don't *do* anything, but I mean . . .

Sophie   Right.

Ann   He's my boyfriend.

Sophie   Yeah. I know.

Pause.

Ann   I'll see you tomorrow, yeah? Are you . . . gonna watch?

Beat. Sophie *nods. Then /*

MOVEMENT

Ann's *pre-race routine.* Sophie *watching. And /*

45

Changing room.

Sophie   Have you *seen the / times?!*

Ann   Yeah! Yeah! / I

Sophie   I mean *fuck*, I mean *how* . . . you / just

Ann   I don't know! I just felt strong and thought I'd push on at the bell, and then I looked up / and

Sophie   Honestly, I thought I was hallucinating! You looked like you were barely moving! *So strong.* Like / *unreal!*

Ann   Ha / yeah

Sophie   1.57.9 are you *kidding*?!

Ann *laughs, grins.*

Sophie   European champ?! What?! I mean where did that even . . . *Fuck!* You're not even tired, / look at you!

Ann   Ha, no I am, I'm / just

Sophie   Seriously, / *fuck*

Ann   Full of adrenaline.

Sophie   That's an insane PB!! *1.57.9* . . . That's . . . You're a *machine!*

Ann *laughs. Grins.* Sophie *stares at her for a moment. Until /*

46

Gym.

Ann   It's not *your* song.

Sophie   It kind of is.

Ann   You can't own a / song

Sophie   No, but I told you about it, / like

Ann   It's *basic.* Everyone knows that song.

Sophie   But I, like I told you that / I

Ann   It's not a big deal.

Sophie   Yeah, but like you say, that in an interview right, and then if I say it . . . it sounds like I'm copying / you

Ann   No one cares about that stuff. It's just a social media thing. They kept saying they wanted more 'content', so . . .

Beat.

Look I'm . . . Sorry. I didn't realise it was a big / deal

Sophie   It's not a big deal.

And /

MOVEMENT

Training. Ann *flying.* Sophie *pushing, until /*

47

Trackside.

Sophie   We could get a takeaway? Mum left me cash. I've found this new route round the back of the / barracks

Ann   Yeah, no, I'd love to but I, we've got a wedding.

Sophie   A wedding?

Ann   Yeah, Si's . . . cousin . . . second cousin . . . once removed . . . dunno. Up in Newcastle. I won't know anyone, it'll be dry, but drinks, dinner, dancing, why not.

Sophie   You're gonna drink?!

Ann   No, obviously not.

Sophie   Well when are you gonna do your long run?

Ann   Sunday evening, or, I dunno, I'll swap with / Monday

Sophie   You have to stick to Paul's programme.

Ann   I am sticking to the . . . I know what I'm / doing

Sophie   But you're not doing / the

Ann   Sophie, / what

Sophie   When are you doing all this training?

Ann   What training? I'm doing the same training as you. I'm doing what he sets / us

Sophie   It's just . . .

Ann   What?

Sophie   S'fine. You do you.

Ann   *What?*

So . . .

MOVEMENT

Ann *trains: focused, free, strong.*

Sophie *examines her reflection: belly, thighs, back; an inventory of every piece of skin, until /*

48

Athletics complex hallway. Quiet.

Ann   Oh. You waited.

Sophie   Well, I . . . yeah. What was that about?

Ann   Um. Yeah, it was . . . it's about the World Championships. Um, the board wanna put me forward. I mean they have.

Sophie   That's amazing!

Ann   Yeah. Yeah, it's nuts. Ha. Said they've been watching me train, race, the Euros, my 'trajectory', they think I've got 'medal potential', whatever that / means

Sophie   Well you do.

Ann *exhales, overwhelmed.*

Sophie   Don't . . .

Ann   What?

Sophie   You got the grade. You've been racing brilliantly. You've literally shot ahead. Plus Osana's out with her hamstring. You know they've been sizing you up.

Ann   Yeah, but I thought maybe for next year, I mean I'm still underage aren't I, I thought . . . I dunno.

Sophie   Well. Bagsie a seat next to you on the plane to Doha.

Ann   You're coming too?!

Sophie *nods*.

Ann   Oh my gosh!

Sophie   Only coz Osana's injured. I'm the wildcard.

Ann   No, you're in coz you're in.

Sophie   I haven't got the grade. I'd have to really kick on to make it past the heats.

Ann   Well, you will. Or . . . let's hope a few more hamstrings go.

Sophie   That's not funny.

Ann   Sorry.

And /

49

Airport.

Sophie   They were doing *last calls*. Paul's been ringing you. They said your name over the tannoy. Didn't / you hear?

Ann   I went to get food.

Sophie   There's food on the plane!

Ann   I wanted something nice.

Sophie   Don't tell me you went to *McDonald's*.

Ann   What?

Sophie   Fucksake.

Ann   Look I'm here now aren't I, queue's barely moving.

Sophie *sighs, but /*

50

Hotel hallway.

Ann   Yeah, I'm fine, I just um. I spilt tiramisu on my shirt so I . . . came back to change.

Sophie   Oh. You missed the opening speeches. You got a mention.

Ann   Did I?

Beat.

Everyone keeps . . . it's a lot of . . . all the media.

Sophie   You're great at it. They love you. 'Rising star.'

Ann *looks like she's going to be sick, and . . .*

51

Hallway.

Ann   Good luck. They really go for it with the needle.

Sophie   Don't say that! You know I get / fainty!

Ann   Ha. Sorry sorry, no, they're really nice.

Sophie *rolls her eyes. Beat.*

Ann   I'm off to bed. Gonna get in the zone. How you feeling?

Sophie *nods.* Ann *nods. Puffs out her cheeks*

Sophie   'Shutthefuckup.'

Ann   Right back at ya.

Sophie   See you in the . . . / morning

Ann   Yeah.

Beat. They get it. Ann *salutes.* Sophie *nods.*

Ann   Sleep well.

Sophie *nods, and . . .*

MOVEMENT

Pre-race prep: night before, morning of . . . warming up . . . tension rising, and rising, then /

52

Hallway. Ann is rushing.

Ann   Did you get called?!

Sophie   Aren't you supposed to . . . you should be warming / up

Ann   I have, I was, but the administrator just called, came to . . . said they want me back in medical / before

Sophie   Why? We have to be in the pens in / like

Ann   You don't have to go back in?

Sophie   What? No, why?

Ann   I don't / know

Sophie   You're meant to be / at

Ann   I know, I know /

But /

53

Stadium. World Champs.

Ann   Have you seen coach?! / Paul

Sophie   Ann, what's / going

Ann   Where is he? Have you seen him?!

Sophie   Why aren't you in your spikes?

Ann   HAVE YOU SEEN HIM?!

Sophie   No!

Ann   Shit . . . / Shit.

Sophie   Ann, you're first heat, you're supposed to be in your / pen

Ann   Please /

Sophie   You shouldn't be here, we're supposed to be in our holding / pens

Ann   Yes, that's why I need . . . Please.

Sophie   What?!

Beat.

What?

Ann   I . . .

Sophie   What?

Beat. Ann *is struggling to breathe.*

Sophie   What? What's going on?

Ann   I don't understand, I don't . . . Ab . . . abnormal, they just said . . . / abnormal.

Sophie   What?! Abnormal / what?

Ann   Result, abnormal result, the blood test they just said . . . I don't . . . I don't get it, / I don't . . .

Sophie   Which blood test? The hormone / test?

Ann   I don't get it, it must be a, a mistake, I . . . I haven't done anything, haven't taken anything I / promise

Sophie   You haven't . . . You / definitely

Ann   No! No. *Of course I haven't!*

Sophie   But, so, the hormone test / it was the

Ann   They just said, they just said too much testosterone, too / much

Sophie   Too much / *testosterone*?

Ann   Yeah and they said, they just said that / I can't run

Sophie   So what you can't, you're not allowed / to run

Ann   There must be mistake! I need to go race! I'm meant to be racing! I'm all warmed up! My heat starts / in

Sophie   Look, / Ann

Ann   I'm meant to be racing! I'm meant to be on the line / in

Sophie   Ann, I need to, I need to be in my pen, my race is in / like

Ann   But /

Sophie   I need to go, I'm so sorry, I have / to

And /

MOVEMENT

BANG! A start-gun.

Sophie's *clock starts and she races.*

Ann's *clock flickers but won't start. She tries to race. Tries again. And again. She panics, looking at the clock, frustrated. It keeps flicking back to zero. She gives up and stands, staring ahead.*

After a while Sophie *finishes, collapsing on the floor, catching her breath. She looks up at the clock, and . . .*

Silence. A silence that seems to go on forever.

Ann *stands still. More silence. Then /*

54

Gym. World Athletics Champs Complex.

Sophie   Jesus / Christ!

Ann   Sorry.

Sophie   No. Sorry. God. Sorry, you just gave me / a

Ann   You were in the zone.

Sophie   It's OK.

Ann   I didn't mean to scare you.

Pause. They stare at each other.

The porter let me through. He recognised me, obviously doesn't know I'm not welcome.

Sophie   What? Of course you're / welcome

Ann   Well, they deactivated my key-card thing. For the whole complex. They moved me off the wing, I'm not in the athlete village anymore.

Beat.

Sophie   I thought you'd gone home.

Ann   Flight's not 'til Saturday.

Sophie *nods.*

Ann   The art gallery's cool. Loads of international stuff.

Sophie   How did you know I'd be in here?

Ann   Raceday eve: sauna; steam-room; stretch. Early one tomorrow right?

Sophie *nods.* Ann *points at* Sophie*'s legs.*

Ann   Don't want them to be uneven.

Beat. Sophie *stretches out her other leg.*

Sophie   I like your hair like / that

Ann   No.

Sophie   Wh / at

Ann   I don't wanna talk about my / hair

Sophie   I just meant it looks nice. It's / different

Ann   Took my racing braids out.

Long pause.

Sophie   Look, I can't even begin to imagine what you're going through, it must / be

Ann   How are you feeling about tomorrow?

Sophie   Er, fine, yeah.

Ann   You ran well in the heats.

Sophie   Thank you.

Ann   Even better in the semis. You broke two. Congrats.

Sophie   Yeah, I did. Thanks I . . . I felt good.

Ann   You looked good. Reckon you're in for a medal?

Sophie   You know I'm not fast enough to medal. I was fastest loser. I scraped / in

Ann   Never say / never

Sophie   I'm not even remotely in the / running

Ann   'Shutthefuckup.'

Sophie   I . . . Yeah. OK sure. Well. Let's see.

Beat.

I should get an early . . . I have to be / up really

Ann   If I raced tomorrow I'd have a proper chance at gold.

Sophie   I know.

Ann   O'Neill's not on form. I've got a better kick than Lopez. The way I've been racing I could get Ferraro on the bend.

Pause.

Sophie   I'm really sorry.

Ann   You didn't even come to find me to see if I was OK.

Sophie   I was racing.

Ann   I mean after.

Sophie   I tried. There was press everywhere, it was mad.

Ann   What about after that?

Sophie   I *tried*, I called you, didn't I? You didn't . . . I did try.

Beat.

Look it was, it's, it's been a shock for me too, OK, I don't, didn't really know what to do with it, I've been . . .

Ann   Jumping for fucking joy.

Sophie   What? No! No / I

Ann   Well, it bumped you up, didn't it?

Sophie   Yes / but

Ann   A-team. In the / mix

Sophie   No, it's / not that

Ann   What?

Sophie   I just think I actually . . .

Ann   What?

Sophie   Well, to be honest I've felt kind / of

Ann   What?

Sophie   Like /

Ann   *What?*

Sophie   Relieved.

Beat.

Ann   Relieved?

Sophie   Yeah.

Ann   You're / *relieved*?

Sophie   *Yeah*. Like. Yeah, like I, ah, God . . . Ann, I've been tearing myself up trying to understand your body ever since I met you! I've been in this for years, inching forwards, bit by bit, and you've come out of nowhere and just killed it! Honestly, I've watched the playback from the Euros over and over and over and over again. When you run you look like you're flying, or dancing, it's effortless, it's *beautiful*. And then there's me with my fat little / legs

Ann   *You don't have fat / legs*

Sophie   Scurrying along, trying to hold on, but no chance.

Ann   Soph, you're through to the final of the World / Champs

Sophie   *Yes,* / but

Ann   You're a world class / athlete

Sophie   Yes, but you're exceptional! You're in another league. I destroy myself, push myself so / hard

Ann   I push myself, train as hard as / anyone

Sophie   But you're sailing towards the Olympics like it's just bound to happen!

Beat.

I've been obsessing over it, trying to work out how I can do literally the same sessions, the same reps, the same circuits, *more* strength and conditioning, *more* steadies, and then it comes to racing and you're three seconds ahead. *Three seconds ahead*, and you've been eating Burger King all week! I've tried eating the same food. Tried copying your patterns. Sucking up any hints I can get like they're secret formulas to success. Thought maybe it was something to do with sleeping, I'm a shit sleeper. And then this comes out, and no, it's *testosterone*. And I'm relieved, of course I am, because I can't do anything about that can I? That's out of my control. I actually think I had the best night's sleep I've had in ages on Monday. And I think I ran so well because I felt like I was allowed to. Because finally, *finally* there was an explanation for why you're so . . . amazing. And I could just focus on me.

Ann *stares at her.*

Ann   I didn't 'come out of nowhere', I've been playing football for *years*. I train fucking hard.

Sophie   I know you do. I know that, I know that, but . . .

Ann   But what?

Sophie   But . . . you know what I mean.

Ann   No, I don't know what you mean actually, I don't know what any of this means, I don't understand where this puts me. 'Abnormal.' Don't fit, don't 'qualify', 'dis-qualified'.

Sophie   Sorry, I / didn't

Ann   The way the board spoke about me in that press release it sounded like I was some kind of mythical creature, some rare species, 'oh, abnormal', she must have magical powers, the elixir of life, 'What's her secret?' 'Blend her up and sell her in a tube for a hundred quid.'

Beat.

They made it seem like I'd done it on purpose.

Beat.

When I was in the gallery earlier I literally paused, I actually *paused* before I went into the ladies loos. Had to take a moment. Isn't that fucked?

Beat.

Sophie   So you didn't . . . I mean did you know? About . . .

Ann   Did I *know* . . .? I . . . I have spent my whole life caught between things. Mum and Dad. England and Nigeria. Religious nut or I dunno, normal person. School or *this*. But I've just been banned, removed, just like that, from the only category I was pretty fucking sure I was part of. It hadn't even crossed my mind that I might not be invited to that party.

Pause. Sophie *watches her in silence.* Ann *turns.*

Sophie   Ann . . .

Ann   Good luck tomorrow.

Sophie   Ann /

But Ann *moves away, and . . .*

MOVEMENT

Sophie*'s pre-race routine.* Ann *stares at her stationary clock. All is quiet, until /*

55

Athletics complex hallway. UK. Ann *is frantic.*

Sophie   You didn't need to do that.

Ann   I / don't

Sophie   You won those. They're / yours

Ann   I don't want them. Not if they don't count.

Beat.

Anyways, look, I've left the box on his desk. He can decide what to do. Give them back to England Athletics.

Pause.

Sophie   Are you here to do the session?

Ann *shakes her head.*

Sophie   You came all the way down just to return / your

Ann   Nah, I'm here to speak with coach.

Sophie   Oh, he's in the gym with the jun / iors

Ann   I know. I went over but all the kids were staring at me / so

Sophie   I'm sure they / weren't

Ann   They were.

Beat.

Sophie   I've tried to call a couple / of

Ann   I think he's mad at me. / Coach

Sophie   Why would he be mad at / you?

Ann   Coz he's wasted all this time. Energy.

Sophie   Ann /

Ann   Sorry.

Sophie   Sorry what?

Beat.

Everyone's been asking after you . . .

Ann *shifts uncomfortably.*

Sophie   Have you been training?

Ann   I'm doing a, like a reception job. Might apply for uni. Or like a / proper

Sophie   Right.

Ann   Maybe I'll redo my exams so I can like apply for a /
better

Sophie   But surely, I mean you don't have to just stop, like
there are options, surely . . .

But Ann *glances to the side, then lowers her head, looking away.*

Sophie   They're not looking at you.

Sophie *watches the people pass. Beat.*

Ann   Yeah, the . . . the board have, um, they have given me
options. If I wanna compete.

Sophie   Hormone therapy, right? To lower / your

Ann   Yeah, and a gonadectomy.

Sophie   A 'gonad / ectomy'?

Ann   That's where they'd operate. Take my internal sex
organs out.

Sophie   Oh. Oh, / that's

Ann   Yeah, and then if my testosterone stays below the limit
for six months I'd be allowed to race. I'd have to be in the
bracket by February if I want to go for Munich.

Sophie   Right. Right . . . and / I mean

Ann   I don't really get it, like I need / to . . .

Sophie   What do your parents / say

Ann   Er yeah, they don't really . . . Like it's, it's a lot. Like
my family, it's a lot for them. Dean's embarrassed, you know,
like everyone at school . . . And Dad won't, can't . . . and like
Mum just keeps praying for me. Wants me to go to the
pastor, thinks I must've done something wrong, or that *she*
must've, you know, like if God loved me then why would he
do this? I mean . . . I don't know.

Beat. Ann *looks around. She is nearly breaking.*

I want to race. I never imagined I could ever want anything this badly. It's all I've thought about, prayed about, dreamt about, this last year. Lanes, lap times, beeps, podiums. Feet hitting the ground. Pad pad pad right across and up and around my room . . . literally chasing dreams across my bedroom ceiling. Legs moving in perfect time. Chasing, chasing, closer and closer. *So close*. Man, I'd've trained through the night if coach told me to. Eaten . . . metal, I dunno. Cut off my head. Coz I *know* I can do it. I can feel it. I *know* I can get faster. I know I can. I could fly. I could *win*. And I like that feeling of knowing I could. I love it. I don't wanna have to let go of that.

Beat.

Sophie   Ann. Go back to Paul's office. Keep your medals. You'll want them one day.

Ann *shakes her head.*

Ann   Medals are just medals, right? Pieces of metal. They can have them. The moments are mine, though. That moment standing on the podium at the Euros? That's *mine*. I can't give that back. And I won't.

A long beat. And /

56

Outside stadium. Ann *sitting.*

Sophie   Were you waiting / for me?

Ann   I saw Carol. She's parked over there.

Beat.

Well run. Coach seemed pleased.

Sophie   I didn't know you were watching. You look well. Have you . . . have you been running?

Ann   Nah. I've been reading.

Beat. Ann *comes closer and* Sophie *flinches.*

Ann   *Wow!* / Are

Sophie   Sorry / I

Ann   You *scared* / *of me*?!

Sophie   No / I

Ann   Wow yeah, forgot I'm a 'threat' now.

Sophie   You're / not

Ann   You worried I'm gonna rape you or something?

Sophie   What?! / Shut up

Ann   Accost / you?

Sophie   Don't be / ridiculous

Ann   'I personally wouldn't feel comfortable sharing with someone who's not a woman . . .' Who said that again? Liz, right? Or was it O'Neill, actually, I can't remember, they've all kind of / merged into

Sophie   I don't / know

Ann   'You can't just put everyone in together willy nilly.'

Sophie   I'm pretty sure O'Neill hasn't said anything.

Ann   Hasn't she?

Sophie   No, she hasn't said anything / about

Ann   Nearly as bad though, isn't it? Keeping quiet? . . . Though on balance I'd definitely say coming out in favour's worse.

Sophie   I didn't come out / in . . .

Ann   I watched the interview.

Sophie   Ann . . . they asked me a question, I gave an honest answer, what did you want / me to

Ann   'Well look it's complex, obviously, but it's all in pursuit of fairness, right? Everyone just wants things to be / fair'

Sophie   I gave an honest and diplomatic / response

Ann   'And the organisers have to draw / the line'

Sophie   'Draw the line somewhere!', yes, because they do! You have . . . You're . . . You have / a . . .

Ann   What?

Sophie   You / . . .

Ann   Say it.

Beat.

Sophie   You have 'a disorder in sex development', right? That's the official / term

Ann   Yep.

Sophie   Right, and . . . and the rules are in place to / protect

Ann   The rules are / bullshit

Sophie   To protect women who *don't have disorders* . . . differences, right? Male bodies, sorry, hormones associated with male . . . with men, with their development, can make people *faster at / running*

Ann   But /

Sophie   What did you expect me to say?! Could I honestly stand there and say that yes, I was happy, perfectly content to line up on the start, to compete in the sport I have spent years, sacrificed *everything*, fucked up school, broken bones for, alongside people who have a *literal* head start? People who, however hard I train, I can *never, ever* beat?!

Pause.

Ann   So . . . so you agree with it then.

Beat.

Do you agree with / it

Sophie I . . .

Ann Do you agree with the ban or not? It's a simple /
question

Sophie Look, if the sports federation people say that this
. . . condition . . . gives people an unfair advantage, if you
have a physical advantage over other women in the group, if
it improves your performance then . . . Look, they have to
have some rules, don't they? If your testosterone levels are
above the limit / then

Ann It's a made up threshold! A number!

Sophie But if they say it gives you an advantage / then

Ann *But they haven't even proven that it does give me an
advantage!* I have partial androgen insensitivity syndrome.
That's how I can have all this testosterone and not have a . . .
penis, OK? It means I can barely use the hormone. And
even if I could, it's not even clear that it would benefit me!
And you know what, even if I they *do* prove that I am
benefitting in some way, then sure, but there are loads of
advantages aren't there? Being tall is an / advantage

Sophie But / that's

Ann Being flexible. Having more fast twitch muscle fibres,
or a stronger heart, or proper / nutrition

Sophie It's a different / thing!

Ann Is it? No one tells someone that their legs are too long,
or their shoes are too good, or they're too, I dunno,
naturally strong, 'sorry Serena your thighs are too / hench'

Sophie That's different!

Ann Why?!

Sophie It just is!

Ann Because it's a sex test?

Sophie   No, because . . . Anyway, it's not a 'sex test', it's an eligibility / test

Ann   It's a sex test.

Sophie   Well, you're not going to help yourself by calling it that are you, if you identify as a girl, / then

Ann   I AM A / GIRL!

Sophie   OK, so don't call it / a

Ann   No one gives a shit what I call it, Soph! They're saying I failed a test to decide whether I'm 'eligible' to compete in the 'female category', so it's a fucking sex test, alright? Don't see any men getting called up for eligibility testing, do you? Too much testosterone? No, they can have all the hormones they want. They can be the hulk if they want so long as it's natural.

Sophie   Well, it's different for / men

Ann   It's always different for men. Michael Phelps with his giant frog feet, mad lactic acid threshold, that skiing dude with his freakish haemoglobin, those mega tall basket-ball guys, but my testosterone's outside the box, so that's it, I'm / out?!

Sophie   Ann /

Ann   And have you noticed something?

Sophie   Can you stop shouting / please

Ann   Have you noticed where these women come from? The athletes who don't fit into these boxes? What they have in common? None of them look like *you*, Soph, I wonder why that / is?

Sophie   OK, / but

Ann   I'll tell you why that is, it's because whoever decided what a woman was, was looking at some skinny European chic, that's why. Whoever gets to draw that blue-print, write up that tick chart, the who's-who of feminine anatomy, has never been to where my mum's from, I'll tell you that.

Sophie   Look . . . I'm / not

Ann   Nigeria. India. Kenya . . . South Africa . . . er / Uganda

Sophie   I / . . .

Ann   Burundi. Namibia . . . And what about the board? What do they have in common? They're all white. All white, and only one woman. The empire might've died but they're still doing a pretty decent fucking job colonising our bodies.

Pause.

Sophie   Look. Ann. I. I'm not saying that this is easy, or, or *right*, I *don't know* what I . . . I'm not supporting it. All I meant was that if we have this rule then there must be a reason. If your body produces an abnormal / amount of

Ann   'Abnormal', excell / ent

Sophie   Argh, sorry, no, I just . . . I just meant there's a reason they have rules, you know, there's a reason we separate men and women in sport, it's so it gives us a fair chance, otherwise we'd never win / anything!

Ann   But why is 'male' what we measure ourselves against?! Seriously, why do women have to exist *in relation to* men?! The moment a woman does anything amazing the first thing we ask is 'is she a man?' Like why is our category defined by theirs? All this 'Oh it's about protecting women', right, sure, but do you know who's really being protected here? By reinforcing these lines?

Sophie   But / Ann

Ann   Men! The patriarchy. That's what wins here. Not us. Discriminating against me is discriminating against yourself, against / all women

Sophie   But . . . / but

Ann   What if they choose a different criteria next? Genitals weren't enough. Chromosomes weren't accurate. They're hot on hormones right now, but what if they start saying you have to get a period every month? You'd fail. Breasts? Questionable. They might decide you don't have enough 'womanly' features slowing / *you* down

Sophie They're not the same / thing

Ann Their categories are bullshit, Soph. I'm living proof. I don't fit. Sex is not binary. It doesn't work.

Sophie But. OK like I see what . . . OK. But I *just meant* that this is *sport*, right? Things have to be fair otherwise there's no point, is there? *It has to be a level playing field!*

Ann *But it's never a level playing field!* I don't know why everyone's pretending that it is! Everything's unfair! Life is unfair! I've never looked out at the girls on the start line of a race, or in a, I dunno, a school, or a train, or in a crowd of people anywhere actually, and thought 'yeah, we're all starting from scratch here, yeah we're about even', life doesn't work like / that!

Sophie But /

Ann But nothing, it doesn't! It doesn't.

Beat.

You know Nike dropped me?

Sophie What?! God, that's . . . really shitty of / them

Ann Well, not much use if I can't compete, am I?

Pause.

Sophie I'm assuming you've decided not to take the treatment then?

Ann It's not 'treatment'.

Sophie No, sorry / I

Ann 'Treatment' is for when people are *ill*. Drugs and operations are for when people *need them*, have something wrong with them. I am fit. I am *healthy*. There is nothing wrong with me. My body works fine. Better than / fine

Sophie   Sorry, I just / meant

Ann   There's no guarantee it'd even work. I've read up about it. Athletes who've done it. They haven't been able to run properly after, it's / fucked

Sophie   Well, surely if the board are suggesting it then it must / be

Ann   Why should I have to be chopped open? Messed with? Take drugs? Change myself to fit with their criteria?

Pause.

When I got the call on Wednesday, about the sponsorship, I . . . well, I needed to get out, like go somewhere. Thought I should buy a pack of fags / or

Sophie   What?!

Ann   Well, that's what people do, right, when things are shit.

Sophie   You don't have to give yourself emphysema.

Ann   Well I didn't, obviously. I just . . . walked. Walked all the way up Staines Road, up to the flyover. Anyway. When I was walking, I was thinking, and I thought about that first time I stayed round yours last year after the Southerns? When Carol drove us back in her Range Rover and she gave us blueberries to eat on the drive? Do you remember?

Sophie *shakes her head.*

Ann   Well anyway, on the way we went past your old school. Those big gates, and the red brick, the tennis courts. Those military buildings with the perfect grass. And when we got in, I remember thinking how soft your carpet was. And the *kitchen*, like that big bit in the middle of it, you know that big marble block / thing

Sophie   The island?

Ann Yeah, posh people have those, right, like what's it even for?

Sophie Well / it's

Ann And your towels, like hotel kinda towels. And all those athletics magazines, and nutrition packs, and photos from abroad, vacations, and your mum all excited, somehow an expert on altitude training. And blueberries in the fridge, ha, like you *always* had them, right, like every time I came over. And I started thinking about how you never really understood why I got stressed about school, why I was worried about my grades. As if there weren't any cracks to fall through, like it was just obvious that life will turn out alright. And then, *then* I thought about what you said in that interview, right? And I thought . . . how comes you get to stand there and say what's 'fair' and what's not?

Beat.

See my faith, my little mustard seed, is something I've had to protect, and grow, and nourish. It's easy for you to have faith, Soph. You get to plant yours in fertile ground. The world has evolved for people like you.

Pause.

Sophie Look, Ann. I'm, I'm sorry, but / this . . .

Ann I'm sorry 'but', great.

And /

MOVEMENT

Ann *cannot make herself train.*

Sophie *trains, slow at first, then harder: grit, pain, mind over matter, straining, harder, harder, until suddenly she gasps: her foot! She crumples.*

A long silence. Then /

57

Ann's doorstep. Hounslow. Sophie *is limping.*

Sophie   Please don't shut the door.

Ann   What are you doing / here?

Sophie   I thought if I told you I was coming, that you wouldn't . . . Sorry. Hi.

Beat.

Ann   Mum's in. We're cooking a big Sunday / dinner

Sophie   OK. Right. Course. Well, if you have to . . .

Ann   No, it's OK.

Sophie   Smells nice.

Beat.

How is Ade?

Ann   She's fine.

Sophie   I thought I'd come after church.

Ann   Oh, I didn't go. Haven't been going.

Beat.

I'm sorry to hear about your foot. Stress fracture?

Sophie   Fractures. Multiple. I was on an easy and it literally just . . .

Ann *makes a face.* Sophie *nods.*

Ann   How long will you be out?

Sophie   Eight . . . ten weeks? Waiting on the reports.

Ann   Well. Good time of year for it. If there is a good time.

Beat. Ann *smiles.*

Sophie   What?

Ann   No, it's just funny seeing you in Hounslow.

Sophie   Ha. The Christmas lights are cool.

Ann   How did you even know my address?

Sophie   It was on that birthday card.

Beat.

Ann   Look, it's cold. I'm letting / the heat out

Sophie   I'm sorry.

Ann   Huh?

Sophie   I'm sorry. Full stop. I'm sorry for not standing up for you. I should've done. I will. I mean I have . . . a bit. / I

Ann   Yeah, I saw the post you did. Appreciate it.

Sophie   I've been thinking about it all. Reading a bit. Well. A lot. I mean I've got time. Like thinking about it / properly

Ann   Yeah?

Sophie   Yeah. *Yeah*, like . . . Like it's mad, isn't it? Like, philosophically I mean. Like, this line we draw, we're obsessed with it, well society is, keeping that division. But that's society, right? Like, not science. And actually, I was reading about a . . . well a tribe, well a few cultures actually where they've never seen just two . . . Sexes I mean. Like they've understood that it's a spectrum, or like a series of . . . states, and yeah it's, like yeah, sorry I'm not really making . . . I just mean it's interesting.

Ann   Yeah, it's interesting.

Sophie   Sorry, I just, I just wanted to say sorry.

Ann   OK.

Sophie   OK?

Ann   What?

Sophie   I. Nothing.

Ann   OK.

Sophie   No, I just. I really am sorry. I want to clear the air.

Ann   OK . . . Sure. Yep. Bit of clear air your side. But it's still pretty murky over here. I'm still being trolled, still getting press requests for weird shit. Comments from athletes in the paper. Creeps sliding into my DMs. People scrutinising my body, speculating as to where I'm hiding my secret dick.

Pause.

Ann   Si's parents don't want him to see me anymore.

Sophie   What?!

Ann   Apparently they're not comfortable with him being with someone who's not 'female'.

Sophie   But that's . . . Oh / God

Ann   He told them they were narrow minded, explained that it's more complicated than that. Well, that's what he told me he told them, I don't know.

Beat.

They said I can't have children. Coz of the . . . yeah. That's more the problem. He wants a family. I mean I do.

Sophie   Oh. God, Ann / I'm

Ann   All this time I've been walking around thinking I knew the shape of myself . . .

Ann *shrugs.* Sophie *moves forwards.* Ann *flinches.*

Sophie   I, sorry, I just . . . wanted to give you a hug.

Beat. Ann *nods. They hug. It's awkward.*

Ann   Look, I er, don't really know what we are, what this / is

Sophie   I'm / just

Ann   This might sound weird, yeah, but I don't really know who you are outside of running.

Sophie   Er . . . ha. Well. Maybe I don't either really.

Ann   Do you even like me?

Sophie *laughs*.

Ann   I'm being serious.

Sophie   I. I . . . Yeah. Of course I . . . Yes, I love you.

Ann   Ha, no you don't.

Sophie   I do.

Ann   But /

Sophie   I do. Like . . . yeah. I mean of course I do, you're my . . . Sometimes I've caught myself looking at you and I've been overwhelmed by ... I dunno, pride, and love, / yeah . . .

Ann   I'm not yours.

Sophie   I . . . I know / that.

Ann   I'm / not yours

Sophie   I *know*. But sometimes I think I've . . . (wished you were).

Pause.

Ann   I've sometimes felt like you . . .

Sophie   What?

Ann   Hate me.

Beat.

Sophie   I'm not sure they're exactly opposites.

A pause, then . . .

58

Athletics complex. Sophie *is fragile.*

Ann   Osteoporosis?!

Sophie   I. Yeah.

Ann   But . . . but / what?

Sophie   It means my bones are fucked. Too long without proper periods. Too much running. Not enough oestrogen. Makes your bones brittle. Amazing I've lasted this long apparently.

Ann   But . . . Shit. *Shit*, so what does that . . .

Sophie   I'm on a rehabilitation programme.

Ann   But I mean when will you . . . when will you be able to run?

Sophie   Um. I think that might be quite a long, um . . . Yeah. I don't know if that's . . . Yeah.

Ann   What . . .?

Sophie   I'm not even supposed to be here. Like, I thought maybe I'd come down to stretch in the gym, just to feel like I'm . . . I don't know what to . . . I think I'm going a bit mad.

Ann   Oh, Sophie, that's . . . / that's

Sophie   Shit. Yeah.

Pause.

You here for the session?

Ann   Just talking to coach.

Sophie   You should say hi to the group.

Ann   Yeah I / dunno

Sophie   They miss you. Seriously, Lyds has been moaning she doesn't have anyone to chase with both of us gone. We need people to push us, right? I mean, I don't think I'd've broken two minutes without you.

Ann   You would.

Sophie   Those mad pyramid sessions last summer? Head-to-head. Sick with lactic. That's the strongest I've ever been.

Ann *smiles. Beat.*

Ann   I should go, Mum's waiting out / side

Sophie   Ann did coach . . . like did he ever talk to you about periods?

Ann   Er. Well, wasn't really part of the chat, was it?

Sophie *shakes her head.*

Sophie   Ha. The medic did ask sometimes. I . . . well to be honest I used to lie. I didn't want them. I used to say I was getting them more often than I did. I didn't want to grow. I wanted to be the smallest, lightest, tightest, fastest version of myself I could be. Take up as little space as possible. Like a little bullet. I loved that feeling. Seeing how far I could push it. Feeling right to the edges of myself.

Beat.

Ann   The medic asked me too. I told the truth. We assumed it was from training. I didn't tell them they'd never started.

Sophie   You didn't tell me.

Ann   I was embarrassed. I kept hoping they would. Kept watching everyone go through puberty, watching myself get left behind. Actually, at running I felt . . . like at high school I was the odd one out, but at running I felt *normal*. It felt like a safe space. I felt right. On the track my body makes sense.

Beat.

Sophie   What's the latest on / the

Ann   The board are being hardline. They've said I can change event. I mean I'm not the only one, am I? They're saying we can retrain, run 2k or 200, but there's no way I'd / qualify

Sophie   That's ridiculous, you're an 800m runner, that's like telling a gymnast to retrain in, I dunno . . . *tennis*. What does Paul think?

Ann   He . . . er, he thinks I should take the op.

Sophie   What? He / actually

Ann   Well, obviously he says it's up to / me, but

Sophie   Paul can go fuck himself, / seriously

Ann   Well, his job is to look after my / career

Sophie   No, his job is to produce athletes.

Ann   Well anyway, I just told him I'm gonna resign from the club.

Beat.

Sophie   Oh.

Ann   I'm gonna appeal. I need the right people around me.

Sophie   Wow! That's / great

Ann   Well, it's not straightforward. Going down the human rights route, it's a long process, could take years. Legal fees. Like the funding . . . well, there isn't any. But I've found someone to advise me. We're making a plan. Fundraising. Mum's gonna help / out

Sophie   That's / that's *great*

Ann   Yeah. Yeah . . . Yeah it is.

Beat.

Now that I'm appealing. Now I'm in. Fighting. Committing to it. If I don't win. If they don't budge . . . Then that's it. I'm out.

Sophie *nods*.

Ann   I thought sport would be this amazing, liberating place . . .

Pause.

Look after yourself, Soph. I hope your rehab goes well.

A pause. And /

59

London train station. Post-collision.

Sophie   Oh / my God!

Ann   Sorry! I didn't / even

Sophie   Sorry, / hi!

Ann   I thought you were just a random / angry

Sophie   No, that's . . . / Hi!

Ann   Hi!

Beat. Speechless.

What / are you

Sophie   Where are you / headed?

Ann   Westbound. Just been at a . . . meeting thing. Where are / you

Sophie   Er, / Eastbound . . .

Ann   Obviously, I meant like / where

Sophie   Oh, well I'm . . . I'm going to a gallery actually.

Ann   A gallery?! Which one?

Sophie   Tate Modern. Never been / so

Ann   You never / been?

Sophie   'There's a whole world out there', / ha

Ann   Ha. You going on your own?

Sophie   No, I'm . . . I'm . . . meeting someone there.

Ann   Like a . . . date?

Sophie   Er. Yeah / actually

Ann   Really?! To the Tate? A Tate / date

Sophie   Well, I / figured

Ann   It's a romantic spot / actually

Sophie   Stop it.

Ann   It is. Lovely view from the top.

Sophie   Well, I dunno, I've never been, have I?

Ann   First date?

Sophie *shakes her head*. Ann *grins*.

Sophie   Her name's Isobel.

Ann   That's cool. It's . . . it's really nice to / see you

Sophie   You too! I've been reading all your stuff.

Ann   Really? You've / been

Sophie   That article was / *amazing*

Ann   Oh! Ha, thanks, I mean which / one?

Sophie   The feature, the big one. 'We must move beyond mental borders to challenge the / physical ones . . .'

Ann   Oh, / ha.

Sophie   It was really brave. Really, really / great

Ann   Thanks.

Sophie   It's all great. The work you're doing. All the media / stuff

Ann   Thanks.

Sophie   How's the appeal going?

Ann   Yeah, we're still waiting. Jury's out. Literally.

Sophie *smiles. Nods. Beat.*

Ann   You look really / well

Sophie   So do / you

Ann   No, I mean you . . . / do.

Sophie   Oh, well I put on quite a lot of / weight so

Ann   Yeah: you look really well.

Sophie   Ha. Thanks.

Beat.

I'm thinking about doing a coaching qualification.

Ann   Really? That's / cool

Sophie   Not quite ready to actually apply yet. Recalibrate.

Ann   You're made of hard stuff, Soph.

Sophie   Ha, apparently I'm made of crumbling calcium actually.

Ann *chuckles.* Sophie *smiles.*

Ann   I mean it, though. You are. I don't think I'd even considered I could get to this level 'til I met you. World Champs? Olympics?! That was like a dream, not something I could actually . . . But you were always so ambitious, so confident, so sure, it's like some of it rubbed off. Belief, or . . . or entitlement maybe, yeah. It's powerful, man. Addictive. That feeling of knowing you can do it. Knowing you can stretch that bit further. Mind over matter.

Sophie   Ha. I dream about that feeling. I literally dream it. The final push to line. Coming 'round the bend onto the straight, totally dead, nothing / left

Ann   The / burn

Sophie   When your legs kind of bypass your brain.

Ann   It's power. Pure power.

Sophie *nods.* Ann *nods. Pause. A train arrives. They watch it come through.*

Ann   Um, that's . . .

Sophie   Yeah I . . . I / should um

Ann   Well, er. Well, enjoy / the . . .

Sophie   Thanks. Thanks. Have a good / . . .

Ann   Thanks.

They hover. Then go their separate ways, and /

Epilogue

'Proud' plays. They tighten their laces. Prepare themselves. Pump themselves up. Then they take their positions . . .

And they run: euphoric, free, swinging over and around the climbing frame; a run which is really a game, a dance, which builds and builds and builds . . .

The cuts! And they stop, breathless. And for a moment they are young again, and free, bleeding hope into the air.

Their clocks run on and on, until /

Curtain.

For a complete listing of Bloomsbury
Methuen Drama titles, visit:

www.bloomsbury.com/drama

Follow us on Twitter and keep up to date
with our news and publications

@MethuenDrama